A view from the DART

A view from the DART

VINCENT CAPRANI

DRAWINGS
DESMOND McCARTHY

BOOKS

First published May 1986 by
MO Books, 12 Magennis Place,
Dublin 2.

Reprinted September 1986

ISBN 0-9509184-4-X

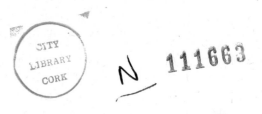
Design: Desmond McCarthy
Origination: Jarlath Hayes
Typesetting: Phototype-Set Ltd., Dublin
Printed and bound in Ireland by Mount Salus Press Ltd., Dublin

Contents

For Mary

Acknowledgements

To all who have helped in this book's production I offer my sincere thanks.

It would be impossible to list all those who so generously offered helpful suggestions and advice, who furnished me with anecdotes and clues and information — various stationmasters, rail employees, DART commuters, barmen, shopkeepers, local historians, passersby — but a special word of gratitude is owed to my beloved wife Mary, as always my constant travel companion and collaborator in writing projects. Her co-operation and encouragement has been continuous and invaluable.

I am also particularly indebted for counsel, suggestions and help to my publisher Derek Garvey, Desmond McCarthy, Jarlath Hayes, Fergus Bourke, Yvonne Nolan, Rory O'Neill, Michael Cullen, K. A. Murray (Chairman and Hon. Ed., Irish Railway Record Society), Donal O Maolalaí (Manager, Public Affairs, CIE), Frank Timmons (CIE), Jim Walsh (Head Librarian, Malahide), Dick Kerr (Dublin Gas Co.), Miss T. Cunningham (Assistant Sec. DSPCA), Richard Nairn (Irish Wildlife Conservancy), Des Keegan and John Markey (Dublin Fire Brigade), Fred Morahan (Bray), Jim Wrenn (Old Dublin Society), Tommy Walsh (Ringsend), Paul Kenny (Malahide), Mr and Mrs Jack Mitchell, Mr and Mrs Dermot Moloney, Jack Caprani, Noel Caprani, Bernie Dwyer.

I herewith express my sincere thanks without implicating any of them in any inaccuracies which may possibly occur in the text or without 'incriminating' them in any interpretation or emphasis which I have given to historical fact.

Introduction

"To hell with the begrudgers. DART is the only good thing our rulers have graced us with in years", claimed one of the national newspapers shortly after the inception of the Dublin Area Rapid Transit system.

I agree. And anyone who recalls the state of rail travel in Ireland during the Emergency years, 1939-1945, will no doubt add a loud 'hear, hear!'. In those years — due to an acute wartime fuel shortage — the cry at every station was for more turf, more timber; anything that might burn. Often there was nothing on hand to fuel the old 'puffing billies'. The newspapers of the day reported such facts as a train taking three hours to travel from Dun Laoghaire to Dublin, a distance of about seven miles, and a passenger train taking 23 hours to cover the 210 miles from Killarney to the capital. There is a story told of a rural stationmaster remarking in wonderment to a colleague: "Here she comes, Mick, right on the day!"

But the DART Rapid Rail System, I have happily discovered, is much more than a boon to the commuters of today or a vast technological improvement on the haphazard methods of rail travel imposed by the exigencies of the Emergency years. Much more.

For many Dubliners it has already taken on the character of a leisure pursuit ... 'an excursion' ... 'great for the kids, like' ... 'a nice bit of an outin', if you know what I mane' ... something to be compared with a day at the Zoo. In other words it has passed the test with the citizens, who — let's face it — are perhaps the world's greatest detractors and the most mischievous critics of all organised activities and systems. DART travel has won a place in their affections and thus will inevitably become one of the city's hallowed traditions. No mean feat. And I have little doubt that very soon it will achieve the supreme accolade of a 'ballad' in its honour — a sort of Irish version of *Funiculi, Funicula,* that joyous melody that celebrated the introduction of the funicular railway at Naples in 1880.

I look forward to whistling such a tune; because I, for one, have 'taken the DART to heart'.

And yet the following pages are not primarily about the new rail system, nor about Dublin. They are rather an account of one dyed-in-the-wool Dubliner's use of the DART system to visit those many places of interest along the rail line, and adjacent to its stations, which appeal to him. The DART (at once offering easy, cheap, comfortable travel) is like a rapidly-moving corridor leading into a sprawling museum — the treasure-house of Dublin city and its maritime environs.

In these pages I have only touched on those things that interest me. There is much more to be gleaned on this electric odyssey — wayside stations that lead off to the worlds of sport, sandy beaches, picturesque harbours, the sea, historic houses, and the flora and fauna of a region still largely unspoiled by the worst excesses of urbanisation and industrialisation. But in touching on my own interests I doubt if it is sufficient to direct the attention of other day trippers, or weekly commuters, in the unimaginative words of a mere statistical brochure or glorified timetable, dryly enumerating the various stations or the riches that may be viewed through the carriage window. A true evaluation of the present Dublin rail route from Howth to Bray can't really be made in terms of DART station names, topographical descriptions or statistical data.

To portray this part of Dublin, to retell some of its stories, is to attempt to define something of its soul — its history, customs, personalities, changing scenery. It requires, I think, an interpretation such as is afforded by the dual medium of a writer's jottings and an artist's sketches.

And I make no apology for my own selection. I enjoy rail travel and I love Dublin and its lore; and I hope something of that enjoyment and love has found its way into this book. If, on the other hand, I have failed to convey my joy in the restless curiosity that can so easily be satisfied by day trips anywhere between Howth and Bray — if I have failed to convince you of my new discovery, and of my voyages of re-discovery — then why don't you buy a ticket at any DART station and find out for yourself?

VINCENT CAPRANI

Howth to Bray

"Howth is an improving port and post town of the county of Dublin, romantically situated on the promontory, known by the appellation of the Hill of Howth, the highest point of which is 567 feet above high-water mark. Here the mails and passengers are landed from Holyhead, without passing the bar of Dublin Bay; and Howth Harbour is the station of the Steam-Packets commanded by Officers of the Royal Navy. These vessels can leave the harbour at any time, and generally arrive at Holyhead in seven hours".

— Leigh's Road-Book of Ireland, 1832.

Alas, within a mere four years of the above description the vessels with their Royal Navy personnel could neither leave nor enter the harbour at will; the port was rapidly silting up. The mail and passenger boats were transferred to the rival harbour of Kingstown, Dunleary. It was a bitter blow to the people of Howth.

There were denunciations, recriminations and no end of 'I told you so' mutterings. Some said the harbour would have been a great success if constructed a little to the eastward at Balscadden (the 'town of the herrings', in Gaelic). Others blamed it on the malevolent envy of the residents of Kingstown. Hadn't the southerners vented their antagonism to Howth's getting the coveted port from the very beginning? They had indeed! When, in 1805, it was first decided to bring the Irish mails through Holyhead to either Howth or Dunleary a fierce controversy developed between the champions of the rival ports.

Howth lost out. The real enemy was the insidious and relentless silt. It strangled the port, choked the commercial hopes of the townspeople and robbed them of their prestigious steam-packets. Within twenty years of acquiring a brand new harbour the 'improving port and post town' had reverted to being a pleasant fishing village.

And, happily, it still retains that character to this day. Take a brisk stroll on the pier after a hearty dinner, or before ambling into the evening warmth of a pub, like the quaint and homely Cock Tavern on Church Hill, which dates back to the 1720s, at least. Then you'll see what I mean.

Howth and its hill is a treasure house of legend and myth and history. Here at the dawn of Irish history the Parthalons and Firbolg lived, mining for ores of copper, until they were subjugated by the Gaels. The latter, with their great iron carving swords, were not long in hacking through the light copper-made swords of the Firbolgs. Criomthain, the first Gaelic chieftain of the locality, had his fortress near the site of the present Bailey lighthouse. From here the doughty Criomthain often sailed with his raiders to Roman Britain to pillage and do battle, while his womenfolk watched from the high green hill for his triumphant return, his vessels laden down with booty and slaves. Fionn and the Fianna too, ever on the look out for approaching war vessels, had a military post here in ancient times. Binn Eadair — to give the locality its former name (for Howth, from the Scandinavian 'Hoved', meaning head, was to come later) — was an ideal place for just such a look out. The summit commands not only a most extensive view of Dublin Bay and the Wicklow Mountains but also the distant peaks of the Mournes, more than sixty miles away; and, in very favourable circumstances — say the clear weather of early morning or calm sunset — the top of Snowdon and the Welsh Mountains can be seen.

And from this summit also were first glimpsed the dreaded longships of the 8th century. Who were these strange new seafarers? Vikings — Norwegians and Danes mostly — large-limbed sea raiders with flaxen hair and eyes of a light blue that were as 'merciless as the deep seas'. For more than two centuries these northern pirates plundered Ireland and in the process established their Viking colonies along the coasts in places like Howth. They routed the coastal Gaels and exacted tribute — the 'nosegelt' — so called from the penalty for default, namely, cutting off the offender's nose. This tribute, and the power of the Norsemen in general, was finally checked by Brian Boru at the Battle of Clontarf (1014) and thereafter the Norsemen kept to their harbour towns where they gradually intermarried with the natives and became integrated in the national fabric.

Then, in 1177, the Cambro-Normans arrived in Howth. They came, not by sea, but riding out from Dublin (which they'd lately seized), a small band of armoured men on horseback, aristocratic in their pretensions, ruthless

Howth Harbour and Ireland's Eye.

adventurers, skilled in the arts of warfare, and lead by the fearless Sir Almeric Tristram. With his mounted warriors, men-at-arms and Welsh bowmen Sir Almeric slaughtered the Danes of Howth near a brook on the hillside which still bears the awesome name of the Bloody Stream. Legend has it that years before, at the shrine of Saint Laurent in Rouen, Normandy, the young Almeric had made a compact of chivalry with his brother knights, each undertaking to achieve fame and fortune by their swords. With just the right blend of religious fervour, romantic chivalry and brutal aggrandisement that passed for valour in his era, Sir Almeric fulfilled his compact against the hapless Irish-Danes at Howth on August 10th, the feast of St Lawrence the Martyr. The victory date, and remembrance of his knightly vows at a faraway shrine in Normandy, were propitious. When the lands of Howth, thus acquired by the sword, were confirmed by King John of England, Sir Almeric thereupon assumed the surname of St Lawrence, the name borne by his descendants to this day.

The splendid castle of his descendants — about 15 minutes walk from the DART station — is a Norman keep of the Middle Ages consisting of battlements flanked by towers, though with some 18th century additions and modifications. It possesses an armoury which contains as its centrepiece Sir Almeric's massive two-handed sword. Think of it — an 800-year-old weapon which in all probability originated in Normandy and which was borne here for the purpose of wresting half a county from its warlike inhabitants!

The grounds of the castle are no less a reminder of Howth's turbulent past. A dolmen in the demesne is said to be the burial place of the beautiful Aideen, who died of grief when she learned of the death of her princely husband, Oscar, slain in battle in 248 AD. There is also a gnarled and ancient tree — called the St Lawrence Tree — which is associated with the legend asserting that one of the Lords of Howth fell madly in love with an exotic and mysterious girl of unfathomable origins who was cast up on the nearby

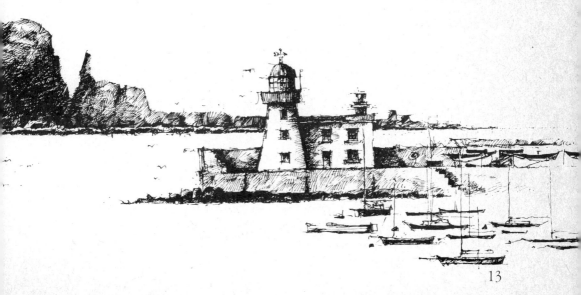

shore by the tide. The castle grounds — open to the public — are however more famous for their rhododendrons. Here, where the sea air has the freshness and substance of heady wine, the textures of either soft rain or rose-gold sunlight works wonders on the countless tones of mauve and red.

And the history of Howth Castle is inextricably woven into the dramatic life story of Grace O'Malley, the sea-queen of distant Mayo. Has any Irish rebel lived more romantically, more colourfully? We glimpse her in situations which link a wind-swept half deck or a square peel tower on the rocky shores of Connaught with the sumptuous London court of Elizabeth I. It was while returning from the London court in 1575 that the daring pirate queen — running before a sudden storm — put into the little harbour under the hill of Howth. Picture the scene, if you will. Grace, a Gaelic princess, naturally anticipates a 'céad míle fáilte' from a fellow noble and hurries towards the castle of milord Howth. But the 'bleak and slitted eye' of Lord Howth, looking down from the graceless Norman castle, is wary of this reckless sea raider from the western seas. The castle gates are quickly locked and armed men suddenly line the battlements. Grace is turned away, at meal time, in savagely wintry weather. She considers this a grave breach of Irish hospitality.

She quickly returns with her hardy clansmen and sailors. There is a lightening strike, a brief but decisive clash of swords — and suddenly the son and heir of my lord of Howth is captured and carried away as a hostage to the O'Malley castle in Mayo. There the boy is held as a prisoner until Grace receives a written pledge from his father that the gates of Howth Castle would never be shut again at dinner time. This condition was observed faithfully by all the descendants of Sir Almeric for more than 200 years, and then was modified somewhat by setting an extra place at the dinner table for any 'unexpected guest'.

At a distance of about a mile from the harbour lies the picturesque little island of Ireland's Eye, the property of the Howth family. About 60 acres of rocky, mountainy land mostly covered by tall ferns it forms a natural breakwater to the harbour. It is uninhabited and its only buildings are a Martello tower and a ruined 6th century church, all that remains of the monastic foundation of St Nessan. Notwithstanding the peaceful and religious associations of its early monastic days the island was the setting for a fearful murder mystery in the 1850s.

There was nothing the solidly respectable Victorians liked better than a good scandal or a vicious murder to add the spice of malice to their after-dinner port and cigars. At a time when fashionable Dubin readers were avidly poring over Gerald Griffin's bestseller, *The Collegians,* with its gripping accounts of the seduction and cruel murder of the Colleen Bawn, they suddenly found themselves with a similar-type killing right on their doorstep, as it were. The murder of pretty 28-year-old Maria Kirwan, and the subsequent trial of her husband William Burke Kirwan, was a *cause célèbre* of mid-Victorian Dublin.

14

On a bright Autumn day in 1852 Kirwan, an artist from Upper Merrion Street, brought his wife to Howth by train for a pleasure trip and picnic. From Howth pier they took a boat out to the island. The sun was high in the sky and warming, there was only a slight breeze. It had all the makings of an idyllic afternoon — Kirwan methodically filling his sketchbook with seascapes and scenery, Maria setting out the picnic things from the wicker basket, lolling about in the deep soft ferns or wandering barefooted on the smooth, glistening sands. They appeared to have the entire island to themselves....

But did they?

In the late afternoon a distraught Kirwan returned to Howth. Alone. He had a sad and fearful tale to tell. While he'd been preoccupied with his sketches Maria had wandered off and had apparently chosen to go for a swim. Much later, when he'd snapped the sketchbook shut, put away his pens and brushes and then gathered up the picnic things, Kirwan had gone in search of her. Maria had vanished, presumably the victim of a tragic drowning accident. How terrible! There was a great deal of commiseration and sympathy with the painter in his grief.

There was also the tiny beginnings of suspicion. One or two mainlanders recalled having heard screams coming from the direction of the island during the afternoon. The cries of a swimmer in difficulties, or something more sinister? Some time later the half naked body of Maria Kirwan was found. A *post mortem* examination revealed that death was due not to drowning but to the body having been penetrated by a sharp instrument, perhaps a knife or a sword-stick or some other like implement. Artists generally carried palette knives or pocket knives for the sharpening of pencils, didn't they? And hadn't Kirwan carried a cane with him as well that day? Could it have been a sword-cane? There was a sudden spate of Dublin gossip concerning the disappearance from the house in Upper Merrion Street of others of Kirwan's relatives.

He was arrested, duly charged with murder and found guilty. Some argued that there had been quite a few discrepancies in the case for the prosecution. Moreover, the police had dug in the gardens at Upper Merrion Street, but no dead bodies had been unearthed. There followed a slight shift in public opinion. It gradually built up into a concerted campaign for a reprieve. Almost at the eleventh hour Kirwan's death sentence was commuted to imprisonment for thirty years. On his release from Spike Island jail in the 1880s, an old and broken man, he went to America and took with him the dark secret of 'the murder on Ireland's Eye'.

Boat trips to the island have always been popular with day visitors from Dublin, as has been the practice of fishing from the pier, or waiting for the herring boats to come in with their catch of 'bargains'. Certainly there is enough enchantment to be found in Howth and on the surrounding heights of Carrickmore, Carrickbrack and Shelmartin to keep not only fishermen but photographers, artists and casual wayfarers well occupied every weekend of the year. 'Howth is the gem of Fingal', wrote Fr Dillon Cosgrave in the early years of this century, 'and may even be described as the most beautiful place near Dublin. Here is the great attraction to a citizen of escape from roads, and the still greater of hills, vales and streams, furze, fern and heather. Writing ninety years ago the historian of the county said of Howth: "Were it within six times the distance from London that it is from Dublin, it would long before this be a diadem of picturesque attraction". All Irishmen of the present day will acknowledge that it has at last become so.'

Howth makes an ideal starting point for my DART wanderings. What I propose to do is to take a window seat on the left-hand, or port side, facing the driver's cabin, and travel all the way to Bray, a journey of approximately one hour. Then, still seated at a left side window, I shall return from Bray to Howth, musing and commenting on what I see en route.

And perhaps this might also be an ideal time to take a closer look at my immediate surroundings. The DART's single-glazed saloon windows —

West Pier, Howth.

through which I shall be gazing for the most part — offer maximum visibility and are free from the irksomeness of condensation due to the train's insulation. The insulation provides good protection against heat transfer too. Thermostatically-controlled line-fed convector heaters are distributed through the train under the seats to keep the temperature at pre-set levels — a far cry indeed from the roofless, open-sided carriages in which Ireland's first rail passengers had to travel 150 years ago!

Those early passengers had also to contend with 'noise, showers of cinders, clouds of smoke and vapour', according to one 19th century writer. My window has inward-opening ventilators, and all panels and flooring are sprayed with a proven anti-drumming material, while the roof and walls have an additional application of 7mm thick material for even further noise and heat insulation. One of the many complaints of the early rail travellers was the lack of adequate illumination. Passenger lighting on the DART is arranged as continuous recessed channels in the ceiling, and one-third of this lighting is battery-fed.

Another gripe was the absence of any type of platform at the old-time stations, which were little more than gravelled strips beside the track. The DART's sophisticated air suspension system automatically corrects level and height to match the platform regardless of the load. And speaking of loads reminds me that over-crowding, cramped conditions and inadequate seating were also high on the list of our ancestors' complaints. The DART carriage provides seating for 72 passengers and, if you include the tip-up seats in the doorway area, then seating capacity is increased to 88. A two-car train with crush load can accommodate approximately 500 people. Seats (moquette-covered and of high fire resistance) are comfortable and spacious, with handgrips mounted on the seat backs.

So then, in such pleasant surroundings all I have to do is settle back, relax, put up my —sorry! Seats are not for feet, and smoking is not permitted on the DART. I quickly return my pipe and tobacco pouch to my coat pocket.

Quite right, really. Who can complain about a directive which operates for the comfort of all passengers?

My journey commences with the DART gliding out smoothly from the Howth platform past the rear of Parson's steel fabrication works, which stands on the site of the old power-station for the famous Hill of Howth trams. Alas, little remains today of what was surely one of the world's most picturesque and quaint tramways; running from Sutton Cross to the Summit — with breathtaking views of the Bailey and across the magnificent sweep of Dublin Bay en route — and then clanging merrily down through gorse and heathery cuttings and past pretty farmhouses to Howth station. The saddest and most touching reminder of the halcyon days of the Howth trams (1901 to 1959) lies back in St Mary's Abbey cemetery — the grave of 'the unknown tram man'. Who was he?

A young Englishman, a track-layer, popular with his Howth workmates, but known to them only by his simple nickname. When he died suddenly he left no clue as to his origins or surname. Unable to contact his family (if he had any), his tramway mates had him laid to rest in the strangers plot and they fashioned a 'tombstone' for him from a piece of grooved tram rail. This humble yet enduring 'monument' can still be seen — to my mind one of the most poignant grave markers in Ireland.

Immediately after Parson's factory can be seen — across the main road to our left, and on the high ground — the spire of St Mary's Church of Ireland church emerging over its necklet of trees, and below, almost in the shadow of the spire, the entrance gate to Howth Castle. St Mary's, which contains a window by Evie Hone, was rebuilt in 1866 on the site of a former church. The building excavations at the time uncovered a quantity of sword blades, fragments of armour, bridles, human bones etc., which are believed to date from the period of Sir Almeric's victory over the Howth Danes in 1177. The entrance gate to the castle was built from the winnings of 'Peep O' Day Boy', one of the most successful horses in the Earl of Howth's racing stables in the last century.

18

Last comes the square and heavily battlemented tower of — no, not some ancient castle! — but a turn-of-the-century Presbyterian church. This most attractive church — local grey limestone contrasting with warm ornamental stonework and red-tiled roof — is an interesting reminder that Howth's first Presbyterian congregations were almost entirely comprised of Gaelic-speaking fishermen from the Western highlands of Scotland who, during the last century, frequently put into Howth harbour for long spells. These Scottish fishermen usually brought their own ministers with them and services were originally conducted in the old Mariner's Hall on the west pier. In the 1890s Lord Howth offered the present site to the growing and indigenous Presbyterian population of the district for the sum of two shillings per annum and a thousand year lease. And the congregation, in a sense, repaid the debt by giving the 'gem of Fingal' a charming example of Gothic church and manse.

Bayside (Baldoyle), Howth Junction, Kilbarrack

*'The name Baldoyle dates from the 9th century when Scandinavian
pirates established a stronghold here. They used it to plunder the
treasure-rich monasteries of Leinster. For almost 200 years, until their
crushing defeat at Clontarf in 1014, Viking longships laden with booty
and slaves sailed into this sheltered creek to the north of the Isthmus of
Howth peninsula. These Danish vikings who settled here were known
by the native Irish as 'dubh gall', or dark strangers, hence the name Baile
Dubh Gall, the Town of the Dark Strangers.'*
— The Villages of Dublin. Jimmy Wren, 1982.

Those Danish Vikings saw the northern seas, not as a daunting barrier,
but as a gigantic invitation which led them to the coastal creeks and isles of
Ireland. They saw the flat arable land lying to the west and south-west of
Howth — the environs of the present-day Kilbarrack, Howth Junction and
Bayside DART stations — as a fine area for colonisation and cultivation.
They spent over 200 years contesting their 'right' to it with the native Irish.
Malachy, King of Meath, had to march south to 'chastise' them, which he did
by burning their settlement at Baldoyle to the ground. Before he could march
north again Sitric Silkenbeard, the Norse King of Dublin, overtook him and
'chastised' him a few miles inland from the still smouldering settlement.
Two years later matters came to a head at the battle of Clontarf. The
Norsemen of Dublin and the coastal settlements, with their Leinster-Irish
allies, ranged themselves against the mighty warriors of Munster and
Connaught led by the aged Brian Boru.

It was one of the bloodiest and most decisive battles ever fought on Irish
soil. In the twilight, when the carnage had ceased, what was left of the
defeated Danes limped back with their wounded to the longships waiting at
Howth and the Baldoyle creek. From there they escaped to lick their wounds
amongst their kinsmen at Carlingford and the Isle of Man.

But they returned, albeit subdued and chastened, and gradually re-
occupied much of their old territory. More than a century and a half later,
when the clank of Norman chain-mail and the thunder of hooves
reverberated across the low fields — what ideal terrain for a small force of
armoured cavalry it must have been! — the last of the Danish chieftains,
Hamund MacTorcaill, went down in defeat.

To the victors the spoils. The Norman method was to conquer, build stout
and graceless defensive towers, have vassals and villeins work the captured
land, and then make an endowment to the Church in thanksgiving to the
Almighty for having blessed the bloody work of sword and longbow. Thus it

Kilbarrack Cemetery.

was that Baldoyle and its hinterland became the grange, or home farm, for the monks of All Hallows Priory. The monks worked the land — 400 acres comprising arable fields, pastures, meadows, gardens and orchards — from about 1200 to 1536, when Henry VIII suppressed the monastery and confiscated all its lands and houses. The only vestige of that medieval era existing to this day is a ruined chapel, built in the 13th century by the monks for the serfs and tenants of the home farm, and referred to locally as Grange Abbey. The ruin, surrounded on all sides by modern housing estates, can still be seen beside some sombre trees on a green sward near the present-day Donaghmede Shopping Centre.

Another interesting ruined church in the vicinity is that of Kilbarrack, formerly the parish church of a seafaring community. The graveyard adjoining it is notable as the burial place of the 'Sham Squire', Francis Higgins, an unscrupulous political adventurer and 'con-man' at the time of the 1798 Rebellion.

The area in general is rich in the lore of that rebellion and the affairs of the United Irishmen. One of their leaders was John Sweetman — the surname suggests Norse ancestry — a member of a wealthy family who owned or leased much of the land which originally comprised the home farm of the monks of All Hallows. The fertile lands of Grange Park, Kilbarrack and Raheny — known as the windmill lands, before steam power displaced wind power — were the great granaries that supplied the Sweetman breweries in Dublin's Hawkins Street and Francis Street. A friend of Tone and the other United Irishmen leaders, Sweetman was also one of those wealthy merchants whose lavish generosity did so much to finance the Catholic resurgence with the relaxation of the Penal Laws. He purchased the site for the Carmelite Church in Clarendon Street and there laid the foundation stone in October 1793.

He was simultaneously laying plans for a rebellion. But the spy network emanating from Dublin Castle had long tendrils, and soon the authorities were on the trail of the conspirators. Sweetman's friend, Archibald Hamilton Rowan, was arrested for distributing a seditious document entitled 'Citizen Soldiers to Arms!'. In his book *Life in Old Dublin,* published in 1913, James Collins recounts the story:

Rowan was fined £500, and to be imprisoned for two years, in addition to find security for his good behaviour. Two months after his conviction he was visited by the Rev. William Jackson, accompanied by the spy Cockayne, the English attorney. At this interview Rowan spoke rather freely about men and things. Shortly afterwards, when he learned of Jackson's conviction and death, he knew that the Government would produce evidence enough to have him hanged, so he decided upon escaping from Newgate, which he did in the following manner: he persuaded one of the officers of Newgate that if he brought him out for one hour he would give him £100. His excuse was that he had lately sold an estate, but that a conveyance executed in prison would be void. He only wanted to sign it outside and then return. The officer accompanied Rowan to his house in Lower Dominick Street (now No. 36) where after a good lunch, he asked leave to bid his wife and children adieu in the adjoining backroom. Rowan had, with the assistance of his faithful Swiss butler, made everything ready for escape by means of a knotted rope tied to the bedpost, and by its aid Rowan got down to the stable-yard, and, turning into Britain Street, rode off to Howth. Rowan thus tells how he got away from Ireland: "But in my acknowledgements how am I to mention the generous, disinterested conduct of the two brothers Sheridan, farmers and boatmen, of Baldoyle, who upon being introduced to me by Mr Sweetman, of Howth, and in possession of the proclamation offering £3,000 for my capture, and knowing me only by name, not only concealed me while sheltering at Mr Sweetman's house, but consented to carry me in their small half-decked fishing boat across the Channel to the coast of France, saying to Mr Sweetman, 'Never fear; by ——, we'll land him safe'. And so they did, in two days, although driven back once from near Wexford to take shelter under Howth."

And what of John Sweetman?

Thirty soldiers, with muskets and bayonets, quickly marched into the brewery office at Francis Street and arrested him. He spent five months in a bleak cell at Kilmainham, four years in an even bleaker cell at Fort George, Scotland, and then eighteen years of political exile on the continent. From Paris he kept in touch with Irish affairs and his brewing interests and, while not a professional architect, so scholarly was his knowledge of art and architecture, that in 1815 he submitted the detailed design from which the Pro-Cathedral in Dublin's Marlboro Street was built. The church was opened in November 1825, but Sweetman (who had finally been permitted to return to his native city in 1820) was too ill to attend the ceremonies. He died the following May.

His friend Rowan survived him by nine years and was buried in the graveyard attached to St Mary's Church, Mary's Street, not far from the grave of Lord Norbury, who hanged so many of the rebels of 1798. Collins says of him: 'The assizes at which he was present were invariably followed by wholesale executions. Utterly reckless of life himself, he seemed scarcely to comprehend how others could value it'.

History is silent about the burial places of the brave Sheridan brothers and Murphy, the third crewman on that voyage of escape. But many years ago I got to chatting with an old-timer by the sea wall in Baldoyle. He first told me of their gallant story and in the telling he spoke their names with a simple yet splendid pride and reverence.

Perhaps that epitaph is enough.

Bayside

At Bayside we come to the first of five points along the line at which the DART system is fed from the ESB national grid (the other points are at Fairview, Sandymount, Dun Laoghaire and Shankill). The main ESB supply is at 38,000 volts A.C. and this is converted and rectified at the five sub-stations just mentioned to give a line voltage of 1500 volts D.C. The DART trains are highly energy efficient. The newly developed 'chopper control' reduces the electricity consumption of the train at cruising speeds, while the electric braking actually generates electricity to feed back into the system. Thus energy savings in the order of 20 per cent result from this method of regenerative braking.

The Crescent, Raheny.

24

Harmonstown / Killester

'Nearly opposite the gate of Artane School is a narrow road called Killester Lane, traversing the old parish of that name, and leading to the Howth Road at the entrance of the once splendid residence of Killester House, where there is still a path called the Nuns' Walk. The Ordnance maps mark a building 'Convent in ruins' not far from this on the Howth Road. There is a modern house called Killester Abbey. The ruins of the old Church of Killester are in the churchyard adjoining Killester Lane. It was dedicated to St Brigid of Kildare. St Brigid's Church was erected recently to serve the newly-built village of Killester. Killester district has belonged for many centuries to the Howth family.'

— North Dublin City and Environs.
Dillon Cosgrave, O.Carm. B.A.

The rail traveller emerges from the DART station at Killester into what at first glance might appear to be a confusing maze of neat little streets flanked by equally neat little bungalows. In reality the traveller is less than five minutes walk from either Howth Road, Collins Avenue or Killester Lane, the main thoroughfares skirting the housing estate. There are over

25

300 of these bungalows, built in 1920 to house veterans of the Somme and Gallipoli and other battlefields of the Great War, and with their occupancy in 1921 Killester ceased to be a rural village and became a populous suburb.

The bungalows have a brisk, spit-and-polish smartness about them, as one might expect of the homes of old soldiers, and they seem to be lined up for one's inspection. Take care! A stranger might get lost marching up and down their serried ranks. Better to nip back and ask the station-master for directions. Or some passer-by....

If the latter happens to be an old man with pathetically straight shoulders and a walking stick — one, alas, of that dwindling battalion of brave veterans — he will point you with soldierly, yet kindly, precision in the direction of the excellent cricket fields and rugby grounds on nearby Castle Avenue. However, if you have time to pause awhile and engage him in chat for a few moments, he, being of a military background, is just as likely to direct you towards Furry Park House ..., 'only a short step beyond. Just off the Howth Road. Many's the time the Black-and-Tans used to raid that place huntin' for Mick Collins.'

Collins, when on the run, often stayed at Furry Park, taking occasional strolls through the woods of St Anne's with his hostess Mrs Moya Llewellyn Davies. The most hunted man in Ireland must have greatly treasured the peace of those morning walks — brief moments snatched from the hectic and terrible times which constituted his short, tragic life — and must have appreciated too the erudite conversation of his brave and gracious hostess. Oh to have been an eavesdropper! Mrs Davies was a fluent linguist, a writer of learned articles under the pseudonym 'Delta', deeply knowledgeable on medical and economic matters, daughter of John O'Connor who had supported the Fenian rebellion, widow of the Welsh lawyer who had steered Lloyd George to the leadership of the Liberal party and, ultimately, to Downing Street; and Collins was the handsome and energetic young firebrand master-minding a successful guerrilla campaign, the finance minister of an outlawed parliament who organised a National Loan to finance a war and set up the machinery of government, a hunted rebel with a price on his head, and soon to be confronting the same Lloyd George across the negotiating table.

Furry Park House, with its beautiful and ancient sun dial, with its reputed underground passage leading to St Anne's House a mile away, is a stage echoing with great events and great people. It echoes too with the laughter of another frequent visitor, W. B. Yeats. The lofty poet was once greatly amused when Mrs Davies showed him Percy French's doggerel on the subject of Queen Victoria's address to her Lord Lieutenant:

"I think there's a slate, says she,
Off Willie Yeats, says she;
He ought to be home, says she,

French-polishing a poem, says she,
Instead of writing letters, says she,
About his betters, says she."

The entrance to the splendid Killester House stood just across the Howth Road from Furry Park. Not a trace of the house remains today — vanished, like the wealth and the titles so greedily sought after and amassed by its former owners, the notorious Newcomen family. Their story is one of brief glory edging over into miserly gloom before finally descending into a squalid tragedy.

William Gleadowe of Killester was an ambitious and unscrupulous social climber, a young man in a hurry to make a fortune, acquire a title and establish a banking dynasty. His first step was to find a wealthy bride, preferably an only child who could be expected to inherit all of her pappa's estate; her looks were really beside the point, and if pappa had good political connections so much the better. William found a Miss Charlotte Newcomen from Carriglass, Co. Longford, an ideal candidate; he wooed, won, wedded and bedded her in 1772.

Within a decade his wife's ample fortune had enabled him to open a private bank in Mary's Abbey, Dublin, her family influence had gained him a seat in the Irish Parliament, her connubial obedience had provided him with a male heir, and William's own single-minded pursuit of self-interest had earned him a Privy councillorship and a baronetcy. For the latter he assumed the name and quartered arms of his wife's family and then, as Sir William Gleadowe Newcomen, he prepared the next step in his grand design. The bank was prospering, so bigger and more imposing premises in Castle Street were purchased; he carried out extensive improvements to Killester House, imported the finest pedigree stock to improve his growing herds, became a most influential director of the new Royal Canal Company and, in short, rapidly amassed even more wealth and prestige. All that was lacking was some bauble for Charlotte. She likewise was not without ambition, and she would have dearly loved a peerage. Could William do anything for her?

The chance came in 1800 when the British Government, under Pitt, were trying desperately to force through the Act of Union. The damnable Irish were once again proving their obduracy, declining to vote their parliament out of existence. At least some of them were. Others were quite prepared to sell their votes providing the price was right. In the great debate Sir William (according to the *Irish Quarterly Review*) 'declared he supported the Union, as he was not instructed to the contrary by his constituents. This avowal surprised many, as it was known that the county was nearly unanimous against the measure, and that he was well acquainted with the fact. However, he voted for Lord Castlereagh, and he asserted that conviction alone was his guide. His veracity was doubted, and in a few months some of his bribes were published. His wife was also created a peeress. One of his bribes has been

27

discovered registered in the Rolls Office — a document which it was never supposed would be exposed, but which would have been found for impeachment against every member of the Government who thus contributed his aid to plunder the public and corrupt Parliament.'

Sir William, it appears, was indebted to the Treasury of Ireland to the tune of £10,000 — some, there were, who reckoned the figure as £20,000 with interest over the previous fourteen years — but Castlereagh had no problem in striking out the massive debt with a stroke of his pen in return for the much needed vote, nor had he any difficulty in securing the much coveted peerage for Charlotte. She became Baronness Newcomen of Mosstown in 1800 and three years later was elevated to the rank of Viscountess. Richard Edgeworth, Newcomen's fellow MP for Longford, and one who had strenuously opposed the Act of Union, wrote bitterly and prophetically:

'With a name that is borrowed, a title that's bought,
Sir William would fain be a gentleman thought;
His wit is but cunning, his courage but vapour,
His pride is but money, his money but paper.'

When Sir William died in 1807 his son and heir, Thomas, succeeded to the Newcomen wealth and titles. Ten years later he inherited Charlotte's estate after her death. Unmarried, described as a 'pervert and reprobate' Thomas had only eight short years in which to enjoy his wealth and status — that is, if 'enjoy' is the correct term to describe his melancholy and miserly existence. Fitzpatrick, in his book *Secret Service Under Pitt,* takes up the sorry tale:

'For years he lived alone in the bank, gloating (it was widely whispered) over ingots of treasure, with no lamp to guide him but the luminous diamonds, which had been left for safe keeping in his hands. Moore would have compared him to the 'gloomy gnome that dwells in the dark gold mine'. Wrapped in a sullen misanthropy, he was sometimes seen emerging at twilight from his iron clamped abode. One day Newcomen's bank broke and prosperous men perished in the collapse. Lord Newcomen had previously retired to Killester, where he perished by his own hand, aged 49. No claimant appeared for his coronet, which became extinct'.

And what of Killester House? It receded into the shadows of history and was left to its sad broodings for almost a century. It flared into prominence only once, briefly and tragically, when, in 1919, it was burned to the ground. The date is not without a peculiar significance: it was the year of the commencement of the Anglo-Irish war which effectively sundered the Act of Union.

Is there a more tragic cameo of the impermanence of political fortune, overweening pride and family ambition than that of the Newcomens of Killester?

Killester and Harmonstown DART stations are very well situated for visitors to nearby St Anne's Park. In either case it is less than ten minutes walk to the Sybil Hill entrance to the park — from Killester station along

Furry Park Road, or from Harmonstown station by way of Sybil Hill Road. An ideal day's outing, or afternoon trip, is to take the DART to either station, enter the park, follow the mile-long drive leading to where St Anne's House once stood — not forgetting to visit the sumptuous Rose Garden en route — and then proceed through the wooded walks to the lower garden and exit gate on the James Larkin Road at the seafront. From there the No 44A (Mount Prospect Avenue) or the No 30 (Dollymount) buses take one back to the city centre, a journey of less than thirty minutes. Bring a picnic basket, and a camera — for the Rose Garden is a delight!

'Flowers are words which even a babe may understand', the American clergyman Arthur Coxe once wrote. At St Anne's the roses recite poetry — with names like *Zephrine Drouhin*, *Blue Moon*, *Alba Maxima*, *Virginiana*, *Silver Lining*, *Honorine De Brabant*, *Old Blush*, *Isaphan*, *Scented Air*, *Nozomi* and scores more, and with every known colour a rose can be, from

iceberg white and pale yellow to the deepest hues of purple crimson. Take a seat for an hour — two, if you can spare the time — in this sheltered, beautifully landscaped and gently-terraced bower; surrender yourself to its rich sights and scents. The combined fragrance of so many roses is a heady mixture, yet peaceful, inducing thoughts like those of Henry Ward Beecher: 'Flowers may beckon towards us, but they speak towards heaven and God'.

St Anne's Rose Garden is a tribute to the combined efforts and the wholehearted co-operation of Clontarf Horticultural Society and Dublin Corporation Parks Department in conjunction with the British Association of Rose Breeders. For more than 25 years the members of the Clontarf Horticultural Society had been visiting all the prestigious rose shows abroad and had been acutely conscious of the fact that their native city had nothing to compare with the rose trial gardens at Copenhagen, Monza, The Hague and Geneva. They took their problem to Dublin Corporation. The Park Superintendent welcomed their suggestions and undertook to provide such a site at St Anne's. As a result Dublin has now joined the select group of cities where Rose Trials are promoted; the Dublin Trials are, however, exceptional in that the roses on trial are the very newest Cultivar Seedlings, still unnamed.

And from the scent of roses to mute, abandoned stones into which tears have seeped....

St Anne's formerly belonged to the Guinness family, Sir Benjamin Lee Guinness bestowing its present name on the old Blackbush property in 1837 and his son Lord Ardilaun bestowing many of the architectural curios which still grace its precincts. The 18th and 19th centuries was an era of 'follies' — towers, obelisks, gazebos, temples, bridges, belvederes, pavilions — as the aristocrat and the *nouveau riche* vied with each other in the production of architectural 'what-nots' throughout the grounds of their estates. The garden walks, the arbours and the pond banks of their demesnes were replete with fantastic flamboyancies of stone. Some of these were merely for 'showing off', others to provide much-needed work for the poor labourers of the locality, and all were intended to decorate their leafy surroundings and to ally art to nature. St Anne's was no exception. Fr Dillon Cosgrave wrote that 'there is no finer demesne within an equal distance of the metropolis, whether as regards extent or beauty'.

At St Anne's there are the scars of vanished buildings; a majestic mansion once stood at the end of the mile-long drive. To the north of where the mansion stood, and abutting an old garden wall, there still remains a 'folly' in the form of a mock ancient temple or pavilion. From the temple a concrete footbridge spans the trickle of the Naniken stream. Some years ago Dublin Corporation erected the bridge, completing a part structure that barely projects in an unfinished state out towards the stream. The incomplete bridge had remained in that state for over eighty years. Why?

On the high ground above the stream, and in line with a path from the narrow footbridge, a scattering of heavy, carved stone pieces lie neglected and untouched beneath the shadows of the holm oaks. It is as if the stone cutter had suddenly and mysteriously stopped work. Vanished. But why?

As a schoolboy I was once told that work ceased on the bridge when the stone cutter was arrested for his part in the Phoenix Park murders of 1882. To date I have been unable to discover the authenticity of this story. What we do know, of course is that one of the four who was subsequently hanged for his alleged part in the killings was Joe Brady, a stone mason and paviour.

Brady was one of eighteen Dublin workmen, all members of a secret society, the Invincibles, arrested in connection with the brutal stabbing of Chief Secretary Lord Frederick Cavendish and Under Secretary Thomas Burke while they were casually walking through the Phoenix Park on a May evening. It was an age when assassination was seen in some quarters as a political expedient — the well-planned murder of a 'notable' might strike fear into the powers-that-be and effect reforms without the necessity of rebellion or a costly war. It was a forlorn, misguided hope. What sort of men were the Invincibles? They were highly respectable, neither rich nor poor,

described correctly as 'nearly all of the artisan class' and with a kind of patriotism which came from emotion rather than intellect.

There is a terrible glimpse of the Invincibles in the dock, silent and grim and vengeful as their erstwhile leader James Carey turns Queen's evidence and informer and points the finger at his former co-conspirators. The *Evening Mail* of February 1883 describes him:

'He wears a peculiarly anxious expression which becomes intensified as the case proceeds. When he enters the dock a sickly smile overspreads his face, but quickly vanishes. By degrees his rather contracted forehead becomes remarkably wrinkled, his eyes look dazed and his cheek bones prominent. In fact, he looks at the close of the day, a broken-down man.'

Carey the informer disclosed all he knew about the killings; from the leading role which he played in the conspiracy he knew virtually all there was to know. Dr Webb, counsel for Joe Brady, harangued him:

'Is your brother, Patrick Carey, among the accused in the dock?'

'Yes.'

'And still you say you are not an informer?'

'I am not. I am giving evidence to save his life, my own life and the lives of innocent men.'

Webb swings round to face the jurymen and cries: 'It was on the knife Carey ought to have been sworn, instead of being sworn on the blessed Evangelists!' He produces pretty young Annie Meagher, who, with her aunt and uncle, give an alibi for Joe Brady at the time of the killings, and he bids the grim-faced jurymen to 'retire and consider who you are to believe — Annie Meagher the pure and stainless, or James Carey, the informer, the hypocrite and the murderer!' But Annie, in addition to being pure and stainless, was clearly madly in love with Joe Brady. The evidence showed it. The grim-faced jurymen chose not to believe her version. Brady, with four of

31

his fellow-conspirators, was executed at Kilmainham Gaol. And Carey — with a new identity, with the Queen's pardon and the Queen's money in his pocket, and with the guarantee of safe conduct and a new life in Her Majesty's colonies — was overtaken on the high seas and vengefully murdered.

The brutal stabbing in the Phoenix Park profoundly shocked Irish society. Parnell was so affected that he offered to withdraw from public life. There seemed to be a national shudder of horror, a conscious desire to eradicate

Furry Park House, Killester.

every trace of the deed and to obliterate every reminder of the names of its perpetrators. In the North Strand area the name of Carey's Lane was changed, and Brady's Row, off Mountjoy Street, was similarly altered. And in St Anne's Estate the erection of a little stone footbridge over the Naniken stream was abandoned...?

The beginnings of the bridge — the solid stone buttress and the merest suggestion of an outward curve intended to arc forward over the brook — all are clearly visible beneath the present concrete footbridge. And on the high ground the shaped stones lie scattered under the holm oaks.

I recently re-visited the site while engaged in research for this book. Unable to resist the lure of old stones I spent some considerable time poking about in the shrubbery and examining the wide-flung fragments of a giant jig-saw puzzle in stone. Practically all of the pieces are far too heavy to be shifted by one pair of hands. I only found one that responded to my efforts to turn it on its side. When I brushed away the leaf mould and the dust of God-knows-how-many years I discovered a clearly and professionally incised set of initials — JB.

Joe Brady?

The hammer and chisel of the stone cutter are silent. There is only the bird song high up among the dark canopy of trees.

Yet how strange to discover quite by accident what may very well be a tangible link with the terrible tragedy of the Invincibles expressed in pieces of unfinished masonry strewn and scattered under the trees of a peaceful park....

Killester to Connolly (Amiens Street)

After Killester we reach the famous 'Skew Bridge' where the railway crosses the Clontarf Road at the north-eastern tip of Fairview Park. Built in 1843 by Sir John McNeill, the great rail engineer, the bridge was regarded as a triumph of engineering at the time. From here the line runs on the original embankment, which was entirely surrounded by water a century ago, but now is all but lost amidst the ever-expanding land reclamation. Part of the easterly, or seaward, reclamation covers the area which was once Clontarf Island. The old maps — Haliday's (1673) and Rocque's (1765) — show the island as a ribbon-shaped piece of land at the confluence of the Tolka and Liffey currents and making a most important and conspicuous object in Dublin Bay.

In the 19th century the island belonged to a wealthy Dublin publican Christopher Cromwell. He built a fine wooden chalet there which he used as a summer residence and weekend fishing retreat. He was staying on the island with his ten-year-old son on the night of October 9th 1844 when one of the greatest storms ever recorded in Dublin suddenly struck with hurricane force. Most of the reclaimed land in the East Wall area was once more under water and waves washed over the roof of the old Wharf Tavern. The roads were impassable. As terrified people scrambled for the safety of higher ground a DMP constable on duty saw the light go out in the wooden house on the little island. The following day, when the storm subsided, the bodies of Cromwell and his son were found on the island shore, retained there by their heavy fishing boots. Their boat had been wrenched from its moorings and carried as far as Annesley Bridge. The wooden house, repeatedly pounded by the waves and the lashing gales, had been demolished

Skew Bridge, Clontarf.

and its timber was strewn along the new railway embankment. It was greatly feared that the embankment, scarcely a year old, might have suffered severe damage in the storm. But on inspection it was found to be intact, a tribute to the work of the unsung rail labourers and the engineer-in-chief, Sir John McNeill.

Immediately after the Skew Bridge, and between the rail embankment and the new Clontarf-East Wall causeway road can be seen the 'toy' road traffic garden where school tots on their tricycles and push-pedal cars learn the Rules of the Road and the rudiments of good traffic sense. Complete with mini-streets, little roundabouts and pedestrian crossings, an attractive and educational playground has been carefully fashioned from a section of the reclaimed land. To the right, at the rear of Fairview Park (itself laid out on more reclaimed land, much of it rubble fill-in from the gutted city centre after the 1916 Rebellion) is the new DART maintenance depot.

The maintenance depot's construction involved the complete demolition of the internal structure of the previous sheds, and rebuilding with new elevated tracks and high-level working platforms. New extensions were built at both the north and south ends, with an amenity block for staff accommodation etc. To provide for additional sidings, new reinforced earth embankments were built at Fairview and further on at Ossory Road, by a method new to this country; it involved embedding strips of galvanised reinforcements in a frictional fill to form a monolithic mass. The embankment was then faced with pre-cast concrete elements to prevent spilling of the fill from the face of the embankment. I sometimes think that a conversation between Sir John McNeill and his team of 19th century workmen and the present CIE civil engineering team would be particularly interesting!

From here to Connolly Station the line runs through the East Wall/North Strand/Amiens Street district — all land reclaimed from the sea and the tidal mudflats over the past two hundred years and once known, for obvious reasons, as Newfoundland. But more of Newfoundland on our return journey.

In 1980-81 Connolly Station got a major facelift in anticipation of DART's introduction, with reconstruction work on the platforms, platform roofing, inter-platform subways, layout alterations and a new suburban entrance brought into use on the site of what was the old GSR terminus. As the DART leaves Connolly suburban station, gliding almost noiselessly out onto the beginning of the Loop Line, over Amiens Street, take a look at the fine old pile of Victorian railway offices on your left and the Italianate tower of the mainline terminal building facing Talbot Street. Though somewhat grimey and faded now, the distinctive railway livery of red brick, yellow brick window arches and dull blue brick band, conjure up a picture of the romantic days of steam. Hard to imagine, isn't it, that inside is housed the entire 'space age' computerised Central Control of today's rail system. The installation of the DART system brought on line a lot of high technology — other systems had been examined as far away as Hong Kong to Newcastle in Britain. European and American Rapid Transit systems were studied and the best elements and combination of technologies were selected for the Dublin project. Designed by CIE the system monitors all train movements, signals, electricity supply and other aspects of the service. The status of all elements is displayed at Control at all times. There is two-way communication with the train drivers, and passenger announcements in trains and stations can be made from Central Control and at local stations. The DART system incorporates the most up-to-date control and safety technology available, including: constant control and monitoring of trains, tracks and equipment by the master computer at Central Control, with automatic warning and failsafe systems; automatic braking if a speed restriction is exceeded; computer-controlled signalling system which includes an in-cab display and audio warning for the driver, plus two-way communication with every driver; and back-up systems for train braking and signalling control.

And the Loop Line? It was opened in 1891 by the City of Dublin Junction Railways to link Connolly (then Amiens Street station) with Pearse (then Westland Row) to prevent the loss to the Dun Laoghaire and Kingstown Railway Company of the valuable mail traffic with England. Up till then the mailbags had to be conveyed by cumbersome horse vehicles through the crowded streets. The project was expensive, involving the purchase of much city property, heavy bridging and the raising of the track at the Westland Row end to clear street traffic. And it was unpopular — especially with those who lamented the crude carving out of the line and the vulgar spoiling of the Custom House vista. In fact, for some, the only popular aspect associated with the new section of rail line was the timely introduction of

Connolly Station.

37

Brady's famed 'Loop Line porter' at a penny a pint less than the other brews on sale in the quayside pubs of the time.

Whereas most of today's suburban localities adjacent to the line developed gradually over the years and in most places accommodated themselves unobtrusively to the existing railway this section was scooped out of a busy city area already in existence for over ninety years. Some fine houses had to be demolished, including No 35 Amiens Street, associated with the novelist Charles Lever. Lever was born here at the residence of his father, James Lever, an English architect and builder employed by Gandon on the Custom House. Thus the line runs through a short stretch made up of scrap yards, business premises, flats, shops, lanes and the like, some derelict and ugly, all higgledy-piggledy and never intended to be viewed at such close quarters by the populace at large. The effect, while not pretty, is certainly of interest — as is so often the case with unprettified things.

To digress for a moment here, let me add that for anyone afflicted with a vigorous curiosity which falls just short of 'nosiness' there is a certain fascination associated with the rear view of people's homes and the contents of their back yards. A sedate, a showy, a bland or a non-commital ordinariness may be presented to the neighbours and passersby out front, but something of a householder's real character and interests are revealed by the manner in which rear paintwork is executed (or neglected?), gardens tended, ladders, tools, coal, logs, bicycles, kiddies' toys and lawnmowers are stored or strewn about.

The 'great outback' is a rich ore field for the guess-worker. How many live in this house? What does the occupant do for a living? This householder is a Do-It-Yourself fanatic; that one, a keen gardener. next door are quite obvious dog-lovers — but who owns the rickety pigeon loft further on, father or son? The rail passenger can always indulge himself or herself in hunting clues. The motorist or main street bus passenger hasn't nearly so many opportunities to indulge a Holmes-like inquisitiveness. Perhaps it should be mandatory for all students of urban development, social behaviour, sociology, demography or whatever to undertake periodic field work projects on the DART. And perhaps too CIE should consider offering an annual prize for the most attractive or best kept rear garden visible from the DART line?

And yet all is not ugliness and waste on this short stretch of the Loop Line. At Frenchman's Lane, which runs from Store Street to Lower Gardiner Street, can be clearly seen at close quarters the excellent use made of an old warehouse which is now the Happy Rambler youth hostel. Do any of the French students who make use of the hostel's excellent facilities ever ponder on the origins of the lane or on their long-dead compatriot who had an obscure thoroughfare in Dublin called after him? The name of the lane is found on Rocque's map of 1756. The same map marks Cezar's Lane, long since vanished, off Frenchman's Lane. Might a Monsieur Cezar have been that Frenchman?

The view from the Loop Line is redeemed by our first sight of the Custom House and the Liffey.

38

Custom House/Loop Line

The Custom House stands today almost as much as a memorial to political chicanery and property speculation — on the grand 18th century scale, naturally — as it does to the architectural genius of James Gandon and the sculptural skills of Edward Smyth. When, in the 1770s, John Beresford (Chief Commissioner of Revenue) and his crony, Luke Gardiner, set about wrenching the axis of Dublin from the Capel Street-and-Castle district to the area in and around the present O'Connell Street they used the arguments favouring the building of a new Custom House as the means of doing so.

Everyone agreed that the existing Custom House near Essex Bridge (built in 1707) was unsound and that the larger boats were unable to come up the river and unload there. But Beresford's recommendation of a brand new building to the east of the city caused a furore. It was violently opposed by those with property and business interests in the Castle-Capel Street hub — more especially when it was alleged that Beresford had a pecuniary arrangement with his friend Gardiner, a person known to own most of the property in the Sackville (now O'Connell) Street area. Both stood to gain immeasurably by the erection of a new Custom House on the site proposed by Beresford.

A coalition of west city brewers, merchants and manufacturers, fronted by the Corporation (of whom many of the aforesaid were members) dashed off a series of petitions and complaints to the Irish Parliament. But Parliament — nicely ensconced in College Green between both rival parties, and probably favouring the idea of a nearby, accessible Carlisle Bridge, which was to be part of the Beresford scheme — gave the cold shoulder to the petitioners. Beresford and Gardiner got the go-ahead, though it was some years before their plans came to fruition. In January 1781 we find Beresford writing to Gandon in London:

'Sir — I have the pleasure to inform you that I have at length obtained an order from Government for the building of a new Custom House ... This business must be kept a profound secret, as long as we can, to prevent clamour, until we have everything secured ... the business is of a delicate nature, and must be managed still with dexterity, having the city (Corporation) of Dublin, and a great number of the merchants, together with what is considered as the most desperate of the mob, to contend with, on this side of the water: and also some persons of high interest and weight on your side, who will make use of every exertion to prevent us....'

The site chosen was part of the North Lotts, a marshy swamp shown on the maps of the day as part of the strand. Beresford's 'profound secrecy' meant delay and it was not until August that the work began. Gandon's diary provides an account:

'On Wednesday, the 8th August, 1781, about sixty feet in length, and fifty in breadth, was cleared out and levelled, and the first stone was laid by the

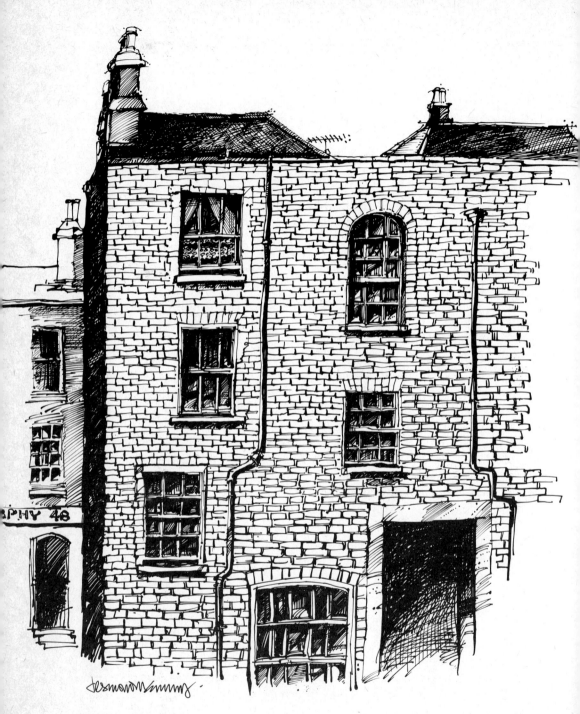

Amiens Street.

Right Hon. John Beresford, without any formality, as we were apprehensive that a riot might be got up by the assemblage of a number of interested persons.'

But the Corporation and its cohort of merchants and brewers were not unduly perturbed. Their experts had scoffed at such a harebrained scheme as a massive edifice built on a quagmire — why, as each new trench of Gandon's was dug a fresh spring of water was uncovered! The whole thing was becoming one of those jokes beloved of Dubliners. Gandon was so busy ordering pumps to cope with the terrific volume of water emanating from the underground springs that he was becoming a laughing stock, a carnival sideshow. 'One Sunday morning' he relates in his diary, 'many hundreds of the populace met on the ground. Whiskey and gingerbread were in great demand. It was apprehended that a riot would ensue, and that the trenches would be filled up; such was not the result; on the contrary, they amused themselves by swimming in them'.

The hard pressed architect left them to their swimming and joking as he burned the midnight oil in his efforts to lick the problem of the underground springs. He eventually came up with an ingenious idea — why not construct the building on a vast foundation raft of fir planks? The plan worked.

When it was learned that Gandon's innovative foundations held, and that the building might after all be successfully completed, the coalition panicked. So they sent in the heavy gang. 'The High Sheriff', Gandon continues, 'accompanied by an influential member of the Corporation, who subsequently became a conspicuous personage, as a military general (Napper Tandy), followed by a numerous rabble, with adzes, saws, shovels, etc., came in a body on the grounds, and levelled that portion of the fence, which had been thrown up, adjoining the North Wall and River Liffey'.

Despite further harassment and opposition Gandon kept steadfastly to his task. It took ten years — 1781-1791 — and a half million pounds to complete the Custom House and its adjoining dock, and a few years later the Carlisle (now O'Connell) Bridge was opened to the public. The commercial and social centre of Dublin lurched eastward. The Castle-and-Capel Street party reluctantly accepted defeat; they even extended a grudging admiration in the direction of Gandon's masterpiece.

For masterpiece it certainly was, making Gandon stand to Dublin as Sir Christopher Wren stood to London, and establishing his reputation beyond doubt. The decoration of the Custom House also established the reputation of a hitherto unknown Dublin sculptor, Edward Smyth. Until the Custom House, Smyth had spent his talents on nothing more exciting than modelling ornaments for chimney pieces and the odd tombstone.

Perhaps the greatest of all Smyth's achievements are the famed riverine heads — the river-gods of Ireland, used as keystones for the arches of the Custom House — each emblematic of the major Irish rivers and distinguishable by means of the produce of their various river banks. For instance, the Liffey, as Anna Livia Plurabella, is a female head, while the Foyle bears a headband with the date '1689', a reminder of the Siege of Derry. There are fourteen keystones in all, the Liffey, Erne, Foyle, Slaney, Nore, Suir, Lagan, Lee, Shannon, Bann, 'Atlantic', Blackwater, Barrow and Boyne. Smyth's excellently-wrought riverine heads appeared on the back of the first Irish currency (pre-decimal) notes.

Smyth also executed the figures of Neptune, Wealth, Mercury and Industry which originally stood above the portico on the south side. These figures were badly damaged by the Custom House inferno of May 1921, and were subsequently removed. What remains of three of these figures found a final resting place in a corner of the Custom House grounds almost directly beneath one of the massive stanchions of the Loop Line bridge. Attractively grouped before some tall shrubbery — and clearly visible from the DART — the group of figures very quickly earned the nickname 'The Three Stooges'. (Dubliners have a penchant for nick-naming their city's statues. Within hours of the unveiling of the effigy of the patriot Wolf Tone — against a semi-circular surround of tall granite plinths at the corner of St Stephen's Green opposite the Shelbourne Hotel — some wag had dubbed it 'Tone-henge').

The Custom House inferno of 1921 recalls earlier fires which caused considerable damage to the building: one in 1798, when carpenters left a

brazier burning after working hours, and a more serious conflagration four years later which caused damage to the extent of £4,000. This second fire at least provided a good binge for many of the onlookers. Originating in the stores, somewhere among the vast consignments of sugar, sulphur, saltpetre and spirits, the fire quickly spread. More than a hundred puncheons of whiskey were tossed out onto the dock in a valiant effort to save them. Or stave them in? Most of them burst open on striking the cobbles, so that 'the dock resembled a huge punchbowl from which watchmen and idle fellows helped themselves to large cupfuls, before this too became part of the blazing inferno'.

This is the first recorded reference to the Custom House being a haunt for idle fellows. Its importance as a headquarters for the collection of customs declined rapidly after the Act of Union, 1800, when Ireland was saddled with the trade restrictions imposed by Westminster, and all custom business (like so much else that had kept the 'second city of the empire' buoyant) was transferred to London. By 1809 Watty Cox's Magazine was complaining that:

'Our Custom House is no use, nor of any importance to any but those idle and greedy reptiles to whose comforts and extravagance it is converted.... Not even the appearance of trade is kept up among the

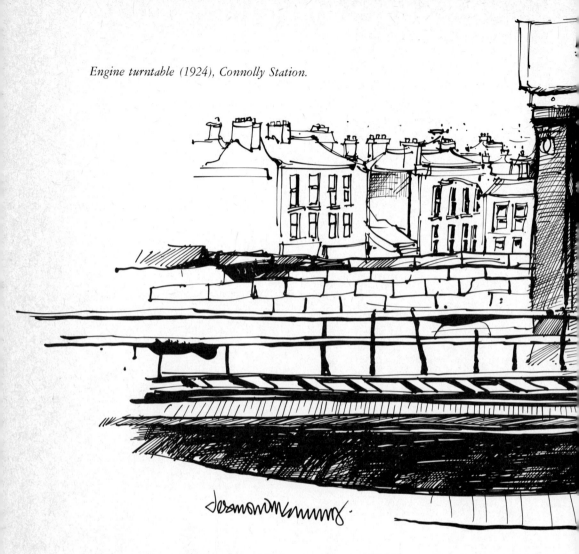

Engine turntable (1924), Connolly Station.

demi gentry who are billeted on this mock Custom House, they despise
the idea of business and the vulgar restrictions annexed to it.'

Beresford, when not residing in his country seat at Abbeville, near
Kinsealy (later the home of Charles J. Haughey, who, as Minister for
Health in the late 1970s had his offices at the Custom House) kept
sumptuous rooms in the fine building which he caused Gandon to build.
In the centre of the northern side was a beautiful room with a vaulted
ceiling which, according to tradition, was Beresford's ballroom.

Thereafter the building became one of the chief centres of British
administration in Ireland. And it was for this reason that the Dublin
Brigade of the IRA was ordered to carry out its destruction during the

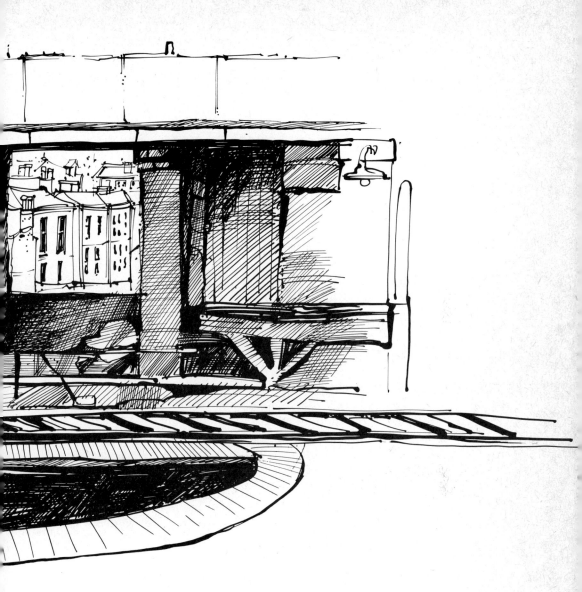

Irish War of Independence, 1919-1921. At 1 p.m. on the 25th May, 1921, two lorries drove up outside the Custom House, each carrying members of the Dublin Brigade armed with revolvers and ominous-looking petrol cans. They rushed the building and placed all the occupants, staff and civilians alike, under close guard while they systematically hurried through the various rooms, sloshing petrol everywhere. When all was ready for the first match the 'prisoners' were given warning and allowed to run to safety. Minutes later the whole place went up in a swoosh of flames.

Auxie lorries and armoured cars were soon rushed to the scene and the Volunteers in the blazing building found themselves surrounded on all sides. Some elected to fight their way out; six were gunned down, a dozen gravely wounded. Some escaped, mingling with the crowd who happened to be in the vicinity. The majority — about 70 men — found themselves trapped in the raging inferno and had no option but to surrender. The loss of so many of the best fighting men in the Dublin Brigade was a serious blow to the IRA. But the burning of the Custom House, which contained most of the records and documents of British government 'symbolised the final collapse of English civil administration in this country', according to *An t-Oglach,* the official organ of the Irish Volunteers.

The ruins of the Custom House, and the immense quantity of books, records and documents stored in it, were still smouldering seven weeks later when the Anglo-Irish Truce was signed on July 9th, and cracks due to cooling were still taking place until the following October.

In the mid-1950s, in the grounds of the Custom House and almost directly opposite Busaras, a memorial was erected to the memory of the men of the Dublin Brigade, Old IRA, who lost their lives in the battle of the Custom House on the 25th May, 1921. Consisting of a fountain, ornamental pond and a bronze statue symbolising Eire consoling one of her fallen warriors, it was financed by funds from the Old IRA and executed by Jean Renard Goulet.

But, somewhat perversely, I still prefer the statues of the 'Three Stooges'. Though battered, broken, fire-damaged and woebegone, they are classical representations of a bygone age that excited the mild derision of the Gardiner Street urchins who so easily christened them 'Curley, Larry and Moe'. As such, they are a kind of monument to the perennial humour of the Dubliner.

And they are not nearly so sad and tragic as Goulet's memorial to poor Sean Doyle and his comrades who died on that Summer's afternoon in 1921....

Dublin owes its existence to the Liffey. Like so many other cities worldwide it was built on the river because of the importance of the water as a highway. And the exact position of the town was determined by the fact that here, only a few miles from the sea, was a place where the river could be forded and then spanned by a wooden bridge. There are now fourteen bridges over the Liffey in the city area, each succeeding one (since the oldest existing bridge of 1776) moving down river and eastward, and drawing the city inexorably in their wake, as it were. To the east of the Loop Line bridge lies Dublin's dockland.

Life is lived lustily in the dockland area. It has little self-contained worlds, which until quite recently had their own distinctive populations, customs, traditions and mode of life. Outsiders who visited it did so rather as explorers in a spirit of adventure, seeking some experience which was not readily obtainable elsewhere. The most noticeable and familiar landmark of dockland is undoubtedly the 250 ft high gasometer on Sir John Rogerson's Quay. Actually 250 ft *6 inches* to be precise! And did you know that the gasometer once had its own little colony of pet mice, and that a luminous white arrow was painted on the top as a directional sign for aircraft?

The white mice were there for the purpose of detecting any possible gas leaks, and they were lovingly tended by gas workers whose safety was to a large extent dependent on the sensitive sniffing of their little pets. During the 1930s the lofty gasholder was an invaluable aid for small planes flying into Dublin, for the white arrow painted on its roof at the request of the Department of Defence pointed the way towards Dublin Airport. The painted arrow was greatly appreciated by aviators flying small planes with few navigational aids. The outline of the arrow, which was painted out during the Second World War, is still faintly discernible to aviators to this day.

Tara St/Loop Line

Is the stretch of the Loop Line railway between Tara Street station and Pearse (Westland Row) the shortest distance between any two DART stations? I certainly think so. And why Tara Street, when the station has no exit or entrance from that street? The station opens out onto George's Quay, in fact.

Yet for such a short stretch there is much to see in the foreground: the not inelegant spire of City Quay parish church, the more ponderous roofline of St Mark's, Hawkins House (on the site of the old Theatre Royal), the darkly-tinted glass of the Irish Press newspaper office (built on the site of the old Tivoli Music Hall, and said by some old pressmen to be still haunted by the ghost of a long-dead actress) and — most impressive of all — the 130-foot watch tower of Tara Street fire brigade station.

I always think that there's something very appropriate in the distinctively Italianate design of the central fire station's conning tower. Present at the official opening of the station on September 13 1907 was Lord Mayor Joe Nannetti, the only Italian ever to hold that much-coveted civic office, and the first Labour representative to be elected Dublin's 'first citizen'. And, moreover, the recently built fire station stood on the very piece of waste ground where Giuseppe Cervi, more than a decade earlier, had set up the first mobile 'chipper', thus giving Dubliners the 'wan-and-wan', a meal which quickly became as popular on the workingclass menu as the more traditional coddle or tripe-and-onions.

In *Ulysses* James Joyce gives us a glimpse of Joe Nannetti and his friend, workmate and compatriot, Tony Caprani, my grandfather. It is the scene where Leopold Bloom enters the caseroom of *The Freeman's Journal*:

'He pushed in the glass swingdoor and entered, stepping over strewn packing paper. Through a lane of clanking drums he made his way towards Nannetti's reading closet ... HOW A GREAT DAILY ORGAN IS TURNED OUT ... Mr Bloom halted behind the foreman's spare body, admiring a glossy crown.

Strange he never saw his real country. Ireland my country. Member for College green. He boomed that workaday worker tack for all it was worth. It's the ads and side features sell a weekly not the stale news in the official gazette.... Shapely bathers on golden strand. World's biggest baloon. Double marriage of sisters celebrated. Two bridegrooms laughing heartily at each other. Cuprani too, printer. More Irish than the Irish.'

Giuseppe Cervi arrived in Dublin in the 1880s, penniless and with scarcely a word of English, having disembarked from an American ship at Cobh and walking from there to the Irish capital. Those old-time Italo-Dubliners — Nannetti, Caprani, Bassi, Deghini, Pacini, Arigho et al — stuck by each other. Work was quickly found for Cervi in Bassi's monumental sculpture and stonework yard, and when the young immigrant had saved

Fire Station Tower, Tara Street.

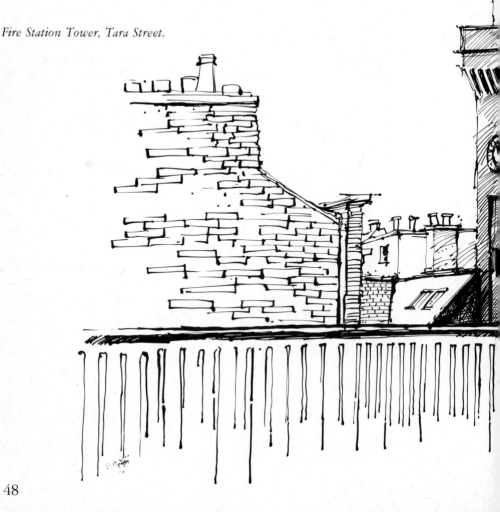

enough to purchase a little push-cart complete with coal-fired cooking apparatus he trundled it over to the waste ground at Tara Street and began to sell his chipped potatoes to the passersby and the pub crowds. As soon as he'd amassed sufficient money for the fare he sent to Italy for the young wife he'd been compelled to leave behind. Shortly after Signora Cervi was joyfully reunited with her husband in this strange, misty city of the north, the couple rented a shop premises in nearby Great Brunswick Street (now Pearse Street).

Signora Cervi, with very little English at her command, helped behind the counter and generally processed the take-away orders by pointing at the selection of fried fish — 'uno di questo, uno di quello' (one of this, one of that). This was soon shortened to 'uno e uno', then 'one and-a one', and in less than a decade Dubliners in general were ordering their portion of chips and one fish as 'wan and wan'.

'. . . Oh John come along for a wan an' wan

down by the Liffeyside . . .'

Ulysses also contains a reference to a well-known fire-fighter of the day, Lieutenant Myers. Myers was second-in-command to the valiant and legendary Captain Tom Purcell, chief of the Dublin Fire Brigade, inventor of one of the first aerial rescue ladders, expert on fire prevention techniques, and the man largely responsible for urging on the city fathers the necessity of a central station at Tara Street. Prior to 1907 the Dublin Fire Brigade (founded in 1862) had its headquarters first in Coppinger Row, then Chatham Street.

Before the formation of the Brigade each fire insurance company

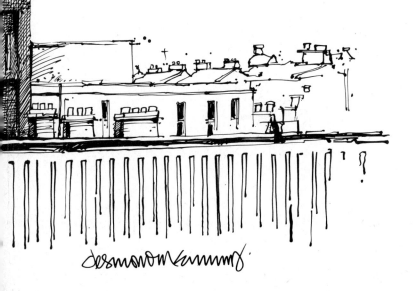

maintained its own engine and staff of firemen. Each company issued its own distinguishing metal disc, which was affixed to the wall of the insured house. When a fire occurred the various insurance staffs turned out and got cracking; but — as frequently happened — if the burning building bore no fire-disc nothing was done. If the luckless building *was* insured, only the firemen of the company concerned got to work. 'This isn't our fire,' the others said and headed back to base, or home. Or the nearest tavern? It was this unsatisfactory state of affairs which lead to the formation of well-trained, full-time fire brigades in the mid-19th century.

And the tall, impressive tower which originally housed a night-long look-out fire sentinel with a commanding view of most of what was then Dublin city — that tower still evokes images of a Tuscan landscape! It is, to my mind, a kind of unconscious but fitting memorial to handsome Joe Nannetti who so ably demonstrated to his compatriots how their adopted town could take them to its heart, and to Giuseppe Cervi with first his push-cart 'chipper' and then his gleaming, brass-knobbed ice cream cart drawn by a handsome black horse with a fondness for pints of porter, and to all the al fresco entertainers and caterers who once occupied the derelict site bordered by Great Brunswick Street and Tara Street and who set the night air throbbing with hurdy-gurdies, hobby-horses, hoop-lahs and the rich distinctive aroma of vinegar-sprinkled 'wan-and-wan'....

Westland Row (Pearse) Station

For me Westland Row/Pearse will always be *the* station. True, there are far more attractive ones in the greater Dublin area; Malahide, for instance, (a frequent winner of Bord Fáilte awards in the past) and the newly-opened commuter stations at Sandymount and Salthill, with their attractive shrubbery beds, cobble-lock paving, modern platform furniture and shelters, all in the distinctive DART livery. But Westland Row/Pearse will always be my favourite — romantic, redolent of history, a vast stage echoing great events.

It was from here — on the morning of December 17th 1834 — that Ireland's first-ever rail engine puffed its way into history, thus irrevocably altering the nation's mode of transport and its economic and social infrastructure. It was, in fact, the world's second true public railroad — the Liverpool-Manchester railway of 1830 being the first; the Stockton-Darlington (1825) and Stratford-Moreton (1827) were originally intended to be worked by horses, but it was the successful adaptation to steam power at Liverpool-Manchester and Dublin-Kingstown in the early 1830s that was to revolutionise the entire public transport system.

The railway's introduction was beset with numerous difficulties. The original intention of the directors was to have the Dublin terminus on the site of Clarendon's Riding School in Great Brunswick Street (now Pearse Street), with the elevated line running near the back windows of the houses in the street and lopping off a section of Trinity College Park, but the opposition to this plan was so effective that the railway entrepreneurs wisely decided to site the terminus at Westland Row. William Dargan built the original station, a neat Georgian frontage in two storeys, the booking halls at street level and a stair leading up to platform level. The builders had little previous experience to fall back on in overcoming many of the engineering problems that thus arose, particularly in regard to the elevated line and the construction of bridges and embankments. For instance, when the first six engines arrived (manufactured and tested at Manchester and Liverpool, then shipped to the Irish capital by the City of Dublin Steampacket Company at a cost of £21 per locomotive) the engineers had to lay sections of portable track along the streets leading from the quays to Westland Row and then run the brand new engines along this temporary railway. At Westland Row gangs of workmen — fifty men to a gang — had to hoist and haul each engine from street level up to rail level.

Then came the problem of the bridges. The Commissioners for Wide and Convenient Streets (the 18th century forerunner of today's *An Bord Pleanala*) which did so much to lay out the elegant Georgian thoroughfares and squares, insisted on having two small side arches for pedestrians added to the railway bridges at Sandwith Street and Great Clarence Street (now Macken Street). The bridges gave Dargan a great deal of trouble as a result of serious settlement. To prevent distortion he attempted to build up the side arches but the Commissioners refused to sanction the modifications and the bridges had to be entirely rebuilt at the contractor's expense, adding the sum of £867 to the original tender. Worse was to follow. As a consequence of an

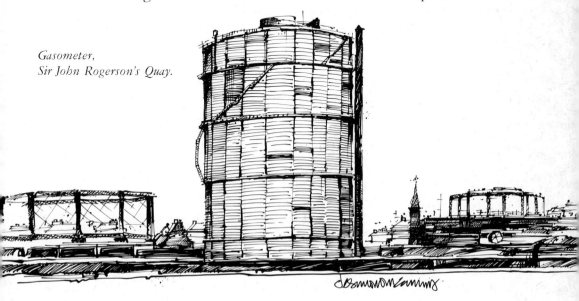

Gasometer,
Sir John Rogerson's Quay.

abnormally heavy rainfall on November 7th — just a few weeks before the official opening of the railway — the Dodder river became very swollen. From earliest times it had a reputation for unruly temperament and frequent flooding, but on that November night it became a raging torrent. Uprooted trees were carried downstream to where a new stone bridge was being built over the roadway at Ballsbridge and where a temporary wooden structure had been erected for the convenience of the public. The uprooted trees, acting like battering rams, smashed through the centering of the new bridge and demolished the temporary structure. The mass of debris rushed down river, gathering momentum all the time, and then crashed violently into the fine three-arched stone bridge newly erected to carry the railway over the Dodder. In no time at all the second bridge came crashing down and was swept away.

Still, Dargan's men had a hastily-built but secure wooden bridge in its place just in time for the opening of the railway. At 9 o'clock on the morning of December 17th the *Hibernia* steamed out of Westland Row station, drawing the first regular train of the Dublin & Kingstown Railway and puff-puffing its acknowledgement to the applause of the many spectators who lined the route. It was filled with 'a very fashionable concourse of passengers', paying one shilling for a First Class Carriage, eight pence for Second, and sixpence for Third Class. Nine trains were run at intervals during that first day, six of nine coaches, the rest of eight, and all 'full to overflowing'. Almost 5,000 people travelled between the inaugural trip at 9 a.m. and the final one at 4 p.m. that day — a far cry indeed from the daily level of 50,000 plus on today's DART!

As befitted the city's first rail terminus — it continued to be so for nearly sixty years, until the Loop Line connected it to Amiens Street — and as the station best suited to meet the requirements of the cross-channel traveller and the mail service with Britain, Westland Row was frequently the setting, or backdrop, for some of the dramatic and colourful scenes in recent Irish history. There are glimpses — vignettes, as it were — of the leading personalities and happenings of 19th century Dublin; O'Connell, Davitt, Butt; and the sombre Parnell quietly pacing the southbound platform and conferring with his colleagues before departing once more for Westminster and the drama of the long sittings and the 'obstruction' tactics. The Kingstown train and the Mail Boat also meant Parnell's reunion with his mistress, Mrs O'Shea — a touching story of deep and passionate love as true and pathetic as it was tragic and disastrous. For the lovers, for Ireland.

And what of the jarveys, the cabmen and hackney car owners, who voluntarily attached themselves to the railway stations to take passengers to their various destinations in the city and suburbs? One such, who had his cab stand at Westland Row, was James Fitzharris, known to all and sundry as 'Skin-the-Goat'. A coarse, cheerful, robust man, Fitzharris had earned his nickname from a tale that he had sold the hide of a pet animal to pay his drinking debts. A police description also described him as 'an ugly, whiskery, jaunty picturesque figure in black overcoat and jarvey's waistcoat and red neckerchief'. Why a police description?

Well, 'Skin-the-Goat' was suspected of being a member of a subversive Fenian splinter group, the Irish Invincibles. He not only plied his cab trade at Westland Row but kept a close eye on the comings and goings at the station of those British officials who were marked out for assassination. And top of the list was W. E. 'Buckshot' Forster, Chief Secretary for Ireland, and chief architect of the coercion policy during the Land War. Viscount Gladstone (son of the great British statesman) writing in *After Thirty Years* states:

'Mr Forster himself narrowly escaped with his life. The Invincibles, knowing that he was to cross by the night mail-boat to Holyhead, literally occupied Westland Row station. The police did not scent danger. The men told off for the deed looked into every carriage. They saw Mrs Forster and the family party. Mr Forster fortunately was not there. He had gone to dine, with his secretary Jephson, at Kingstown'.

Thus Forster narrowly escaped death by a last minute change of plans. A few days later his immediate successor Lord Frederick Cavendish — on his very first day in Dublin, and while walking from the Castle to the Chief Secretary's Lodge in Phoenix Park, in company with the Under Secretary Mr Burke — was brutally struck down by the assassins in broad daylight. 'Skin-the-Goat' had conveyed some of the killers to the park in his cab, and had waited nearby to assist in their escape.

Viscount Gladstone provided a kind of postscript:

'The tragedy of the Phoenix Park (May 6, 1882) was the outcome of the police weakness to which I have already referred. That so widespread and deadly an organisation should have been developed without the slightest knowledge of the police is almost incredible. There was known danger for the chief Government officials and particularly for Mr Burke — a strong, high-minded man who was thought to have the reins of coercion in his hands. I once asked him whether he carried a revolver. "No", he replied; "If they want to get me they can." With their deficient knowledge the police chiefs, thinking the danger was passed, relaxed vigilance in personal protection. So Mr Burke fell a victim to his own courage and public spirit, and with him Lord Frederick Cavendish — beloved of all — who died to save his friend.'

Fortunately such grim, cloak-and-dagger happenings were a rarity at Westland Row. Pomp and pageantry was more the thing, especially for the periodic royal and viceregal toing and froing twixt London and Dublin via Kingstown. For such august jaunts the directors of the railway provided everything from arches of welcome spanning the line to illuminations, special reception rooms, decorated platforms and — the *piece de resistance* — a gorgeously re-constructed Royal rail carriage.

For the visit of Queen Victoria in 1849 the directors were in a real dither.

There was no problem with buntings, bands and illuminations, that sort of thing — why at Westland Row the illuminations were the last word! — an ingenious display of windows edged with gaslights and, surmounting the facade, a large representation of a locomotive outlined in gas-jets and with the wheels actually revolving. No, their real problem lay in procuring a suitable coach for Her Majesty and the Prince Consort.

S. W. Haughton, the Carriage Superintendent, came up with the bright idea of completely re-building and furnishing one of the latest 'wide' four-compartment coaches. The available time was short, yet in little over a fortnight Haughton's men produced a veritable 'palace on wheels' with the carriage interior being rearranged in three divisions — vestibule, saloon and an ante-room for the ladies-in-waiting. The central saloon, almost 12 foot long, contained settee, chairs and footstools, all upholstered in light blue tabinet to match walls draped in the same material and colour and patterned with shamrocks, roses and thistles; the ceiling was a profusion of white and gold arabesque ornaments, the floor richly carpeted. Four line mirrors reflected a stand of fresh flowers centred on a gleaming table; the plate glass windows were framed with curtains of white damask embroidered in gold. The vestibule and ladies compartment were of a similar, if more muted, elegance. Nor was the coach's exterior lacking in that effulgence of ornamentation so beloved of the Victorians — perpendicular lines of royal blue on white, with the royal arms and those of the City of Dublin emblazoned on the centre panels. The smaller panels were not overlooked either — they had wreaths of the ubiquitous shamrocks, roses and thistles, with mottoes and the Queen's monogram. Even the roof of the carriage was decorated with the royal arms, crowns on tasselled cushions and a scroll bearing a motto in execrable Gaelic, *Céad Míle Fáilteach*.

Grand Canal Dock

From Pearse Station the down line crosses first Sandwith Street, then Erne and Macken Streets, passes the carriage sheds and Boston sidings before reaching the interesting three-span skew bridge over the Grand Canal. On the right is the tall, gaunt Guinness malt store; on the left the dark waters of the Grand Canal Dock. It can be a grim looking place, especially on a cold wintry morning. More or less deserted now, its bleak warehouses and mills are reminders of 19th century freighting and industry.

The area is not all railway sidings and freight depots, a composition of dark shades and industrial outlines devoid of those many-hued decorations which brighten the face of a residential quarter. There are very attractive 'villages' of the new town houses, clean, diminutive and pretty, and the warm red-brick of the IDA centre and the sparkling grey-white granite of the old Hammond Lane Foundry tower block, now face-lifted and renovated and housing the IDA craft centre which was recently awarded a Europa Nostra diploma by European conservation bodies. It serves not only as an impressive landmark and as an old building restored to functional purposes but as an excellent blueprint for other neglected buildings in need of regeneration.

At Grand Canal Street there is another sight that never fails to gladden my heart, for here I can look down into the boarding kennels of the Dogs and Cats Home, run by the DSPCA, and be reminded of one of my favourite books, *The Story of San Michele* by Axel Munthe. In the 1920s and 30s the book was a bestseller in 25 languages. There is something infinitely touching in Dr Munthe's words:

'To become a good dog-doctor it is necessary to love dogs, but it is also necessary to understand them — the same as with us, with the difference that it is easier to understand a dog than a man and easier to love him. Never forget that the mentality of one dog is totally different from that of another. The sharp wit that sparkles in the quick eye of a fox-terrier, for instance, reflects a mental activity totally different from the serene wisdom which shines in the calm eye of a St Bernard or an old sheep-dog. The intelligence of dogs is proverbial, but there is a great difference of degree, already apparent in the puppies as soon as they open their eyes. There are even stupid dogs, though the percentage is much smaller than in man. On the whole it is easy to understand the dog and to learn to read his thoughts. The dog cannot dissimulate, cannot deceive, cannot lie because he cannot speak. The dog is a saint. He is straightforward and honest by nature.'

Dr Munthe, an eminent nerve specialist in Edwardian times, sought a cure for his insomnia by writing *The Story of San Michele,* went blind before it was half completed, then recovered his sight, and donated most of his royalties to organisations for the benefit of the blind and animals. He once said 'My happiest moment was when the Isle of Capri, where I live, was declared a bird sanctuary and the trapping of birds was forbidden. I valued them more than my sight. I have derived as much happiness from the companionship of birds and animals as from human beings'.

The Dublin Dogs and Cats Home was established in 1885 after great efforts to raise funds and to find suitable premises. Mr Barlow Kennett guaranteed £500 for a Dogs' Home at the time on condition that a similar sum was raised by the DSPCA, and that the same amount, on the same condition, was found for a Cats' Home. A Miss Swift undertook the organisation and administration of the Cats' Home, first raising the necessary money and then generously endowing the home on her death some years later. With the passing of the Dogs Act in 1906 the Home became the pound for stray dogs and to this day remains as the only official police pound in the city.

The Home stands today not only as a shelter and hospital for stray dogs, injured horses, donkeys, rabbits, guinea pigs, hedgehogs, ferrets, fox cubs, hamsters, gerbils, wounded gulls, pigeons and swans 'oiled' by Dodder spillages etc., but also as a kind of monument to 'Humanity' Dick Martin, to a Mrs Thompson who, in 1837, established the Irish Society for the Prevention of Cruelty to Animals, and to the generations of concerned animal lovers who formed, and continue to assist, the work of that organisation.

Martin, born in Dublin in 1754, was a wealthy landlord, a witty eccentric, an excellent horseman, an expert swordsman and a fearless duellist. His skill with pistols earned him his first sobriquet, 'Hair Trigger Dick'. But his lifelong concern for the poor and the under-privileged and his reforming zeal earned him the later and more enduring nick-name, 'Humanity' Dick. As MP for Galway at Westminster he worked tirelessly to expose the cruelties inflicted on dumb animals. It was an age of bear-baiting, cock fights, dog battles, and of overworked and exhausted horses being whipped into the crude slaughterhouses of the major cities when they were no longer of use to their owners. There the horses and donkeys were left without food or water until their time came to be brutally hacked down. Martin visited such places, knew at first hand the cruelties inflicted, and fearlessly exposed the evils.

In 1821 Martin presented a Bill in the Commons which proposed that any person having charge or custody of 'any horse, cow, ox, heifer, steer, sheep or other cattle' who ill-treated them should be brought before a magistrate. Defeated, he re-introduced the Bill the following year and was successful.

Grand Canal Harbour.

Over the next four years he endeavoured to bring in similar bills to protect dogs and cats, to suppress cruel sports and to improve the appalling conditions in the slaughterhouses. He was instrumental in establishing the first SPCA, combing the streets and alleys of London to seek out and bring succour to wounded and neglected animals. He supported Wilberforce's crusade for the abolition of slavery and was in the forefront of the campaign to have the criminal laws reformed. Such tireless and selfless work cost him dearly. Neglect of his vast estates in the west of Ireland, and of his business affairs in general, put him heavily in debt. The loss of his parliamentary seat in 1826 deprived him both of his immunity from creditors and a forum in which to plead the case of all dumb creatures. Forced to quit London, and then his beloved Connemara, Humanity Dick was obliged to live in France, where he died of poverty at Boulogne in 1834.

Richard Martin's life's work, together with Axel Munthe's words, must appeal with great force to all animal lovers. The animal shelter and boarding kennels at Grand Canal Street continue the spirit of Martin's work of prevention and alleviation of animal suffering, and the Richard Martin Restfields for the rehabilitation of sick and/or disabled horses and donkeys surely deserve our support.

The premises of the Dogs and Cats Home had previously belonged to the Dublin Sugar Refinery Company and before that had been a brewery, both businesses sited at the canal harbour so as to take advantage of the waterway freighting facilities.

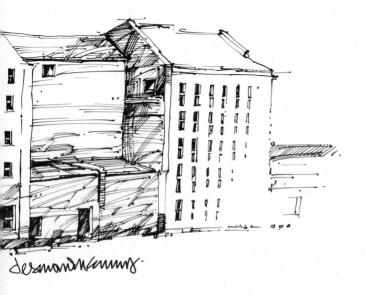

In 1796 the Grand Canal Company opened the suite of docks known as Grand Canal Harbour, thus connecting the Shannon and the Liffey via their canal. There is a romance in sea and river borne commerce which generally compensates for the sombre aspects of the districts which are its inlets and outlets. I have earlier described the harbour as grim-looking, especially on a grey wintry morning. This might have continued to be my abiding impression had not my wife, seeing the canal harbour bathed in warm sunlight one Summer evening, drawn my attention to its colours and opined that its placid waters reflecting the rich, weathered stones of old buildings put her in mind of a Venetian backwater. Somewhat fanciful, I thought inwardly, until quite recently I overheard one teenage DART traveller remark to her companion "Oh look! Isn't that just like Venice!". Her schoolgirl companion agreed with all the infectious enthusiasm of youth. And so now I have to concede that three females marvelling at wavelets breaking gently on brown stones — and above the waterline old buildings grouping themselves as if to conceal a secret from me! — cannot be entirely wrong.

Certainly from the opposite side — the drawbridge on the Ringsend Road — and looking south-west towards the Dublin mountains on a sunny evening, there is a golden haziness about the little harbour which, if not Canaletto, is a sight to dispel any sombre thoughts. Visible from the DART, that drawbridge can be raised to allow craft a passage to and from the Liffey. Many years ago it was the scene of a ridiculous and amusing incident — a collision between a tramcar and a two-masted sailing vessel! River mishap or road accident? It conjures up pictures of a hilarious cock-up — 'Stand by to go about, there's an electric tram bearing down on our starboard bow!'.

The harbour, once the embarkation point and the home port of a fleet of inland freight barges, recalls too the Dublin urchin's taunt to a strutting bargee pacing the deck in the manner of a deep-sea mariner (and in all probability voyaging no further than Portobello or Inchicore): 'Hey, Cap'n — bring us back a monkey!'. Those poor bargemen had to take a lot of stick. Lampooning ballads, known as Grand Canal epics, were *The Cruise of the Calabar, The Wreck of the Vartry* and *The Thirteenth Lock,* for which it was said that the statesman Arthur Griffith was the author.

The harbour and its immediate surroundings are associated too with Bolands Mills and the earlier Dock Milling Company. It may come as a surprise to some people to learn that the once-extensive Bolands Mills started out as a modest bakery shop in Capel Street back in the 1820s owned by Patrick Boland. The premises were extended by his son in 1867 and the extensions included additional ovens built over the area once occupied by St Mary's Abbey. Six years later the Flour Mills at Ringsend Road, once known as 'Pims Mill' were acquired. The famous bakery at Grand Canal Quay was built in 1874, and the old-established Dock Milling Company in Barrow Street was taken over in 1933, when an all electric up-to-date plant with a drying capacity of 190 tons a day and a normal weekly output of 300 tons of flour was installed. The bakery, which became a public company in 1887, attained a certain historical prominence due to its occupation by the Volunteers during the Easter Week Rising, 1916, when Eamon De Valera was in command of the garrison there.

And after Grand Canal Dock, comes Barrow Street. Here can be seen Dublin's trio of 19th century gasometers, or holders, each with a capacity of approximately 3 million cubic feet of reserve stock gas. The Barrow Street gas holders, like the more prominent and better-known gasometer on Sir John Rogerson's Quay (which was built by Dexter's of Manchester in 1934) have been in continuous use since the first one was erected in 1871. The holders are like a giant cylinder with a piston inside; the gas is under the piston and the pressure of the gas lifts the piston right up to the top of the holder. As gas is released during the day to feed the system the piston comes down again. This helps to explain something which used to puzzle me — the constantly varying height of the Barrow Street containers. Take note of their daily 'up-and-down' positions and observe the mechanical wheels attached to the ornate outer supports which operate to raise and lower the massive gasholders.

Immediately after Barrow Street comes the pair of bridges at South Lotts Road and Bath Avenue. Originally, in 1834, it was intended to have a single bridge here, but engineering problems necessitated building two, the first almost square-on, and the second a genuine 'skew' bridge of 33 degrees — and both so low that in later years no double-deck tramcar or bus could pass under them. It is interesting to note that when the line was being altered for the DART changeover the masonry arch bridge at Bath Avenue was demolished and a new bridge built and opened to traffic within a time span of only 36 hours.

Pearse to Lansdowne Rd/Sandymount

'From the Ancient Calendar of the Records of Dublin, in the year 1454, we find a decree of the Corporation ordering all people of Irish blood to quit the city within four weeks under the threat of imprisonment on refusing to obey the order. These homeless victims, both clergy and lay people, made their way eastward to the seashore where they established a community at what became known as Irishtown.'
— The Villages of Dublin. Jimmy Wren, 1982.

'The River Liffey divides Dublin into two nearly equal portions, which may be denominated the North and South Divisions,' Leigh wrote in his *Road Book of Ireland,* 1832. Until the advent of the railways — and, indeed, for almost a century after, it might be argued — the river acted as a kind of natural frontier between northsiders and southsiders. In the last century, and in addition to the separate and distinct classes of citizens based on social and religious differences, there was something of a geographic division too. To the majority of northsiders the south city and its environs was almost as foreign as the Sahara desert and Timbuctoo; and north of the river, as far as most southsiders were concerned, might well have been Ultima Thule. Villages such as Irishtown, and particularly its sister parish of Ringsend (almost entirely surrounded by the waters of the Liffey, the Dodder and the sea) were remote and distinct places.

Much of that distinctiveness still remains among the hardy, warm-hearted dockland and seafaring communities of Ringsend and Irishtown. Jimmy Wren informs us that 'by 1660 there were 59 persons of English and 21 of Irish descent living at Ringsend village'. Thereafter, as the chief place of embarkation and disembarkation for the port of Dublin, the area had much commerce with the maritime towns of Britain. An old salt in Dwyer's pub once told me that 'Raytown' — to give Ringsend the nick-name by which it is affectionately known to its denizens — is inhabited largely by the descendants of Devon and Cornish fishing families who sailed there to escape the attentions of the notorious Royal Navy 'press gangs' in the 18th century. Hence the decidedly nautical character of the locality. Irishtown's St Matthew's Church, built in 1703 for the seamen, has a fine belfry — and even finer vaults which were quickly utilized for storing the contraband lace, the kegs of brandy and Rhenish wine hauled in by the local smugglers. An interesting connection this with the tale of the old salt, for in Devon and Cornwall the vicarage cellars and church belfries traditionally provided the hiding places for the forbidden goods until the Preventative men and the

Revenue cutters had gone elsewhere in their search for contraband.

One of the natural benefits of the locality, as described by a writer 150 years ago, is 'the purity of the air, which tends greatly to promote the health and comfort of the inhabitants'. And in his memoirs the patriot Wolfe Tone recalls one of the rare, brief and tranquil periods in his short and tragic life as follows:

'My wife's health continuing still delicate, she was ordered by her physician to bathe in salt water. I hired in consequence, a little box of a house on the seaside, at Irishtown, where we spent the summer of 1790. I recall with transport the happy days we spent together during the period; the delicious dinners in the preparation of which my wife, Russell and myself were all engaged; the afternoon walks; the discussions we had as we lay stretched on the grass. It was delightful.'

Such delightful moments were, alas, all too seldom. Tone's political ideas kept pace with the events and progress of the French Revolution. He made no secret of his espousal of the ideals of Liberty, Equality and Fraternity, of Paine's the Rights of Man, of the principles of democratic government and

St. Matthew's Church, Irishtown.

national sovereignty. He was compelled to flee to America, then Paris, where he took a commission in the French army. His subsequent capture at Lough Swilly, his courtmartial and his death in a felon's cell are part of Irish history. His friend Tom Russell, who had helped prepare 'the delicious dinners, was hanged five years later for his part in Robert Emmet's rebellion.

The bracing sea breezes of Irishtown/Sandymount and the revolutionary air of republican Paris are also intermingled like a whiff of gunpowder and cordite with the story of two other Irish rebels, James Stephens and Charles Kickham. Both were Tipperary men and Fenian conspirators who lived incognito at Fairfield House, Sandymount, for a couple of months in 1865 while Dublin Castle spies tried to ferret out their whereabouts. Stephens's alias of 'Mr Herbert' was in all probability suggested by the fact that Fairfield House stood at the junction of Herbert Road and Newbridge Avenue. Whether or not Kickham affected the alias of 'Mr Newbridge' is uncertain, but the Castle spies were nonetheless active. As a dawn light seeped in from the sea a strong force of detectives quietly surrounded Fairfield House and captured the Fenian leaders.

Stephens escaped from Richmond Prison while on remand. Disguised as a grubby-faced deck hand on a Howth collier he made it to France, and there began his second long period of exile. Kickham was not so fortunate; he was sentenced to fourteen years penal servitude. The veteran Fenians — one the author of the still popular novel *Knocknagow* and the other the translator of Dickens's *Martin Chuzzlewit* into the French language while a political émigré in Paris — were to be reunited twentyfive years later when Stephens was eventually allowed to return to Ireland. He settled in Blackrock, near Kickham's home at St John's Terrace. A near neighbour at 11 Warrington Place, Mount Street Bridge, was the third member of the Tipperary triumvirate of the IRB, John O'Leary, another former exile in Paris.

Irishtown and Sandymount are the sister parishes of Ringsend. I say 'sister' advisedly. It would be facile and fanciful to liken any two of them to twin brothers solely because of their closeness, their resemblance and their seafaring ancestry, and far too easy to view them as grizzled old salts sitting by a low quay wall with penknives, whittling wood and fishing nets across their knees. I do not know where one parish officially ends and the other begins. Nor do I care. Events have shaped them in much the same way, one with the other, and they seem to have more of the brave patience and compassion of women waiting and looking out to sea for the return of loved ones than that quality of garrulity associated with old sailors. Behind the raucous pubs and the dockland slang there is a dignity and a comeliness. You doubt me? Then visit little side streets like Stella Gardens. Look at the old, low houses and their postage stamp front gardens. When you see them for the first time you may be forgiven for thinking that the occupants must keep all the paint manufacturers and seed merchants of Dublin in business by their efforts alone. The little houses and gardens are so incredibly pretty that they instantly give the lie to the notion that this is an area inhabited only by rough seamen and hearty dockers.

It is certainly an area of sportsmen and sporting traditions — footballers, wrestlers, tug-o-war men, athletes, oarsmen — and in the 18th century Irishtown and Sandymount Green were popular venues for hectic hurling matches; there is a record of a championship game held here in 1757 between the local batchelors and the married men for a 50 guineas prize. Indeed, it would be hard to find any city in the world which could be described more aptly than Dublin by the epithet, 'a sporting town'. Napoleon once described the English as a 'nation of shopkeepers'. If he had not been deterred by the line of twentyone Martello towers dotting the coastline from Skerries to Bray he might have discovered that the Irish are a nation of sportsmen. At such times as the All-Ireland Gaelic football and hurling finals, the rugby internationals, the Irish Open Golf Championship or the Irish Derby are taking place the average Irish man — and woman — has time for little else. News of national and international importance, no matter how earth-shattering, is swept off the pages of the newspapers to make room for sports reports and commentaries. A foreigner or a latter-day Napoleon might be intrigued or easily startled by such headlines as 'Dublin in Danger!' or 'Ireland at Risk!', only to discover that the dire catastrophes are nothing more serious than the possibility of a local sporting defeat. As for horse racing, the 'sport of kings', it is probably the most popular of all. With flat-racing from Spring to Autumn, and hurdling and steeplechasing from Autumn to Spring, there is a kind of twelvemonth sporting festival in which scarcely a family in the land hasn't some financial interest in the results, even if the wagers are nothing more than 'a few bob each way'.

Today the Dublin sporting fraternity is well catered for by a number of convenient race courses and sports stadia, two of which — Shelbourne Park and Lansdowne — are in the Irishtown/Sandymount area. In fact DART travellers actually alight from the train almost beneath a modern two-tier sports stand straddling the station and the railway line at Lansdowne Road — the mecca of Irish rugby and a regular venue for international and European Cup soccer matches.

Lansdowne Rd (Ballsbridge)

'Ballsbridge and Donnybrook, in the county of Dublin, are situated on the Dodder, and the latter is celebrated for its great fair, which commences August 26th, and lasts for six days. Here the native humour of the Dublin citizens is annually displayed when, after accustomed libations, the word is followed by the blow, a well tempered method of making good the most brilliant points of Irish wit and argument. The sale of horses of every description adds considerably to the spirit of Donnybrook Fair. In this village are cotton-printing Mills, and a Hospital for Incurables. The ancient Church deserves notice.'

— Leigh's Road-Book of Ireland. 1832

The Fair, established by King John in 1204, gave a new word to the English language — a 'donnybrook', meaning a riotous free-for-all or mêlée. Originally Donnybrook Fair ranked high among the great European fairs as an important trading centre, with merchants travelling from many foreign lands to transact their business on the banks of the Dodder. By the early 1800s the Fair had lost most of its foreign visitors and many of its more respectable craftsmen as the great Dublin bare-knuckle prizefighters Dan Donnelly, Jack Langan and Andy Gamble set up their booths and challenged all and sundry to 'step out with the raw 'uns'. Fist fights, more often outside the ring that in it, became part of the attraction. The fair was finally abolished in 1855 because of the riotous behaviour. The Lord Mayor of Dublin asked, and was granted, low rail fares in compensation for the abolition of Donnybrook Fair. And the abolition owes as much to the new found respectability of the neighbourhood as it does to the incidence of faction fights at the livestock fair. The 'quality' were moving into the Ballsbridge and Donnybrook locality in greater numbers.

It was during the years 1860 to 1886 that the face of Dublin's residential areas began to take on the familiar shape seen today. Before that a trot around the perimeter of the city would have been no great endurance test. It was roughly equal to two laps of the present Phoenix Park, and on the 3,600 acres were all the worthwhile buildings of the capital. The cathedrals, the Castle, the Georgian houses of the vanished aristocracy, the factories, the plants operated by the various trade guilds — even the tenements towering astride cobbled streets — were all squeezed between two rivers, the Dodder and the Tolka. The Liffey carved its way eastward to Dublin Bay right through the centre of all these buildings.

Between the 60s and 80s of the last century Ballsbridge and Donnybrook emerged as well planned sections of wide, tree-lined roads with the now familiar red-bricked houses fronted by impressive gardens. The development, especially around Ballsbridge, had necessitated the re-building and widening of the original bridge over the Dodder, and had seen the growth of a rather narrow belt linking the area with Blackrock and Dun Laoghaire. But Ballsbridge has always meant more than a residential area or a topographical boundary. It has, like Rathgar, come to signify a mode of living. Quality was the keynote here — respectability, fine houses, fine manners, rules and regulations of conduct not formulated by any written code. Things were 'done' or 'not done' in areas like Ballsbridge. Its denizens regarded themselves as much more than mere Dubliners, and they had a distinctive accent — quite unlike the nasally twang of the true Liffeysider — to prove that Ballsbridge stood for the cult of elegance and luxury. For a long time the spirit of Queen Victoria and her serious-minded consort reigned in the area.

When, in 1851, Prince Albert focussed worldwide attention upon a vast and lofty structure made entirely of glass and iron, and known as the Crystal Palace, the Dublin Victorians felt encouraged to dutifully follow the example of their betters. London's Crystal Palace had been the venue for a mammoth international industrial exhibition. Could the Dubliners hope to match that? To be called, as it often was, 'the second city of the Empire', gladdened the hearts of the Dublin Victorians; but despite this flattering title no one with sense could ascribe to their city the distinction of being an industrial metropolis. In those days it was to a large extent the capital of an agricultural nation. Were it not for its thriving breweries and its distilleries it would not have been even on the industrial map with Belfast. So, they would just have to settle for an agricultural show and exhibition.

The first show held at Ballsbridge in 1871 was under the auspices of the Royal Agricultural Society of Ireland. These shows were held during August alternatively in the four provinces, and the Ballsbridge show of 1871 became the forerunner of the subsequent RDS Spring and Horse Shows. The VIPs attending its opening ceremony must have similarly gladdened the hearts of the leading families of Ballsbridge — men such as the Prince of Wales (afterwards King Edward VII), Prince Arthur, Duke of Connaught, the Marquis of Drogheda, the Marquis of Waterford, the Duke of Leinster, Lord Lurgan (owner of the famous greyhound 'Master McGrath'), Sir A. E. Guinness (afterwards Lord Ardilaun), Alex Findlater, Sir John Power and Ian Frank Hamilton. The galaxy of international show-jumping stars since then continues to gladden the hearts of Irish sports fans and horse lovers. The annual Dublin Horse Show — with its spectacular centrepiece, the Aga Khan show-jumping competition — has become one of the brightest gems in the diadem of international equestrian events; and the extensive grounds, pavilions and exhibition stands of the RDS at Ballsbridge are a worthy and fitting monument to the fourteen men who, in June 1731, established the Royal Dublin Society 'in order to promote improvements of all kinds'. The society's 250-year contribution to promoting improvements in agriculture, veterinary science, stock breeding, show-jumping, fishing, chemistry, geology, botany, craft work, music, art and literature has left Ireland with an incalculable debt.

Lansdowne Road (formerly Haig's Lane, from the name of a distiller whose plant stood beside the Dodder) got its first railway station in July 1870. The station was opened in anticipation of the forthcoming Royal Agricultural show and to meet the wishes of a rapidly burgeoning high-class residential area. The district was part of the vast Pembroke Estate of the great Fitzwilliam family. The Estate offered to pay half of the estimated £1,200 for building the station on the understanding that if the enterprise was successful profit-wise then the railway company might pay that half and own the station. The locals made good use of the station from the very beginning, the profits increased, and the company paid up as arranged and took possession.

The success and popularity of the subsequent annual shows at Ballsbridge meant too that the RDS could extend its many activities into the railway sphere. In 1893 the Society laid out sidings and platforms for the ever-increasing Show traffic on a short branch line just beyond the Dodder from Lansdowne Road station. A large space was chosen on land which had once been the Spafield Nursery Gardens of Thomas Bridgeford.

Bridgeford was the leading figure amongst all those tenants of the Pembroke Estate who felt aggrieved by the disastrous Dodder floods of 1834, '38 and '39. His gardens had been devastated by the rising and turbulent waters. And he blamed everything on the new-fangled railroad — the level crossings, the embankments, the rail bridge over the river; in short, all this infernal tampering with the natural lie of the land. In 1840 he took the rail company to court and won the verdict, with damages set at £300, but the jury failed to agree that the Dodder bridge — its destruction on the night of November 7, 1834 has already been mentioned — was the real cause of the flood damage. For their part the railway directors (while stoutly maintaining that their business could hardly be expected to prosper if constantly menaced by lawsuits arising from something beyond their control, such as river floods) nonetheless agreed to build an embankment, together with a flanking footpath, along the eastern side of the Dodder between Ballsbridge and the railway. Everyone was happy — Bridgeford, the other gardeners, the locals, and the railway directors, the latter managing to give the appearance of civic-mindedness to their desire that the erratic Dodder should be channeled and guided on its course without further damage to the railway.

The 1893 RDS branch line at the Dodder reminds us too that more than forty years later a somewhat similar, if minor, arrangement was effected for the Irish Hospital Sweeps in the form of a private exit/entry gate for Sweep personnel on the platform at Lansdowne Road station.

Today, considering the DART maximum speed of 100 km per hour and the smooth, powerful acceleration and braking from zero to 60 km per hour in just twenty seconds, it's interesting to recall that the line between Lansdowne Road and Merrion was something of a 'speed trial' stretch for locomotives in the 1830s, before the railway was officially opened. One such test, with an engine using 'bad coke' and having built up a head of steam, achieved a record high speed of 48½ miles per hour along this section of the line.

Lansdowne Road (under West Stand).

Sandymount Station

The new Sandymount DART station — surely one of the most attractive on the line? — stands on the site of an earlier station; or rather on the site of a long series of stations dating back to 1835. It — or they? — have had a curious, chequered, 'on-and-off' history, which seems to have been bedevilled by the competition presented by alternative modes of transport.

The pleasant seaside village of Sandymount, with its sparsely populated hinterland, communicated with the city centre by means of hackney cars, farm vehicles and pedestrian power throughout the early years of the 19th century. Then came the railway. It was convenient and useful, though the trains stopped at Sandymount Lane only once in every three hours. Still, it was an improvement. But even this scant service was discontinued in 1841 despite the wishes of the 'Committee of the Barony of Dublin for Combating Excessive Taxation and Improving the District'. The Railway bosses — James and Thomas Pim, Tom Bergin, Charles Vignoles et al — had discovered that it was no easy job to make money on the stations nearest to Dublin and in areas of low population.

With the exception of one single day — August 6, 1849 — Sandymount was to be without a station for nigh on twenty years. Why August 6th? Well, that was the day Queen Victoria made her first visit to Ireland. She landed from the royal yacht at Kingstown with the prince consort and her entourage, boarded the sumptuous royal rail coach already mentioned, then (with the engine *Cyclops* puffing and belching with self-importance) proceeded up the line beneath the swaying banners, the garlands, the buntings and the arches of welcome to Sandymount. A special flower-bedecked platform had been erected there for the royal halt. From there, after the usual effusions and pomposities, the queen's party went on by road to Dublin.

That one-day re-opening of the station rekindled local agitation for a more permanent arrangement. After all, went the argument, if the railway bosses could go to all that trouble for a few one-day trippers — albeit royals — why couldn't they re-open that station for the regulars? Nothing came of it. It was the era of profit-making, not public service.

Yet still the Sandymount area grew, with more houses going up year after year until, in February 1860, the company deemed it advantageous to finally accede to the requests of the locals. The station was re-opened. Alas, it was another short-lived affair. Demands for a Sydney Parade station had equal weight and when one was opened there in May 1862 the authorities decided to once more close down Sandymount. There was another spate of angry protests, but all to no avail.

Another twenty years passed. The agitation continued, though muted.

Then, in March 1882, the station was suddenly re-opened to the great delight of the Sandymount residents. It was a delight that lasted a decade or thereabouts, for, with the advent of electrified trams in the 1890s (and the resultant competition for fare-paying passengers) it was decided to close the station again in September 1901 to allow trains to make better overall times. More 'give us back our station' demands followed, or, failing a prompt re-opening, then at least the construction of a footpath from Sydney Parade station. That wasn't too much to ask, was it? It seems it was — both requests were turned down on the grounds of cost.

Sporadic calls for a re-opening of the station fell on deaf ears for the next quarter of a century. Then fate intervened. After almost a hundred years of erratic rivalry from hackney cars, private coaches and electric trams the company now found itself faced with the threat of competition from the operators of private bus companies in the motorized era following the First World War. It was decided to meet this new menace by re-opening both Sandymount and Merrion stations in 1928. The latter did very little business and was closed down in 1933, but Sandymount was to enjoy its longest uninterrupted period to date, over thirty years from 1928 to 1960, despite reduced services, the fuel shortages of the Second World War and a steadily falling business. In the late 1950s the policy of favouring road transport as against rail resulted in the station's fourth — many felt it to be the final — closure in 1960.

However, I prefer happy endings. And picturesque Sandymount station

Shopfront, Sandymount Green.

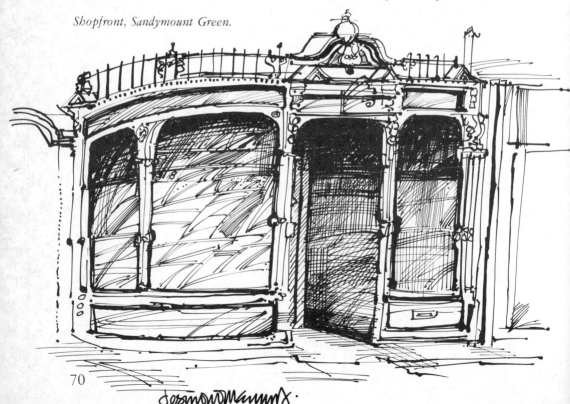

deserved a better fate than total oblivion. It was most heartening to learn that with the proposed electrification scheme the re-use of Sandymount was included in the overall DART plan. Its accessibility and popularity with commuters since its 'fourth' re-opening in 1984 augurs well for the future and assures rail travellers of its continued use well into the 21st century.

I'll settle for that.

And what of Sandymount itself?

I once stopped a passerby in Sandymount Green to enquire the whereabouts of a certain street. "Sorry, I'm a stranger here myself," he replied; and then, somewhat surprisingly added: "Well, not really a stranger. I live in Glasnevin, you see. But I nearly always come here when I'm at a loose end, or feeling a bit depressed. Sandymount never fails to cheer me up. I love its ambience".

He was right, of course. Sandymount has a certain ambience. The Green is one of the few places still remaining in Dublin that retains a kind of recognisable 'village' centre. The 'village' pivots on the tree-shaded, iron-railed Green, which contains a bust of one of the more celebrated writers associated with the area, W. B. Yeats, who was born in Sandymount.

Other prominent writers who dwelled at Sandymount at various times were James Joyce, Frank O'Connor, Mary Lavin, T. C. Murray (the Abbey playwright), while patriots and politicians — James Stephens, Charles Kickham, Eamon De Valera and the brothers Pearse — were also residents at some stage in their eventful lives. The Pearse brothers lived first at Newbridge Avenue, then Sandymount Avenue, and later Lisreaghan Terrace, during the time their father was an 'upwardly mobile' church stone-cutter intent on carving out increasing affluence and social status.

Yet Sandymount Green is a rather bizarre sort of 'village' all the same, possessing as it does something akin to a Hollywood studio set in the mock battlements and lancet windows of Castleton House and the adjoining Castleville. The film industry impression is further heightened — and the Green greatly enhanced — by the Edwardian finery of the Sandymount House pub, and, right next door to it, the carved wooden frontage and the curved windows of a 19th century shop which is like something out of a Toulouse-Lautrec poster. Older residents of Sandymount still occasionally refer to this shop as Miss Milligan's Hardware Store, though it has in its time been everything from a flower shop to a bookstore. Until quite recently the original curved glass windows were pock-marked with bullet holes dating from the 'Trouble Times', a tribute to the durability of the oldtime glassmakers' craft, and to the fact that their perfectly curved panes were able to withstand and to spread the impact of the bullets.

Alas, what the snipers' bullets failed to do back in the 1920s the accidental slip of a carpenter's hammer in the 1980s did — during repair work to the gracefully rounded window cill an upward stroke of a mallet shattered the glass. The present replacement pane of curved and transparent perspex —

while suitable and not incongruous — says as much for the passing of old craft skills as it does for the adaptability of modern substances. Perspex or no, Miss Milligan's Hardware Store has rightly been described as 'one of the most beautiful shopfronts in Ireland'. Whenever I pass it I cannot help think that Synge must have had it in mind when he wrote that 'men cease to build beautiful churches when they have lost happiness in building shops'.

And I cannot help think that the builder of the shop that adorns Sandymount Green probably went on to fashion a cathedral, such was his artistry and his sense of the fitness of things.

Sandymount Green impresses the visitor as a place nestling comfortably and sedately between the rail line on one side and the traffic of the Strand Road on the other. Sandymount Strand — about fifteen minutes walk from the DART station — affords a wonderful view of Dublin Bay, from the Hill of Howth, the Pidgeon House and the 2,000 ft. chimney stacks of the ESB generation station on the left, round to the misty spires of Dun Laoghaire and Dalkey on the right. Its miles of low tidal sands are a feeding ground for the red-billed shelduck, Brent geese, dunlin and wigeon, the latter species the most numerous duck found here with numbers in excess of 3,000 wintering annually at the Bull Island and Sandymount. At low tide the waders can be seen grubbing around the remains of the old bathing place stuck out in the middle of the sands like a deserted wreck, a reminder of the days when the railway ran cheap excursion trips for the 'privilege of bathing free of charge at any of the Company's Cold Sea Baths, on week days only'.

The Pidgeon House — not 'pigeon', as some Dubliners imagine! — derives its name from the first overseer and caretaker of the Poolbeg lighthouse, erected at the furthest extremity of the South Wall breakwater in 1767 and, incidentally, the first lighthouse in the world to be illuminated solely by candle power. Pidgeon resided in a strongly built wooden house close by the lighthouse and supplemented his official income by converting part of his home into a popular hostelry and as a base for running boat trips around the bay. Eventually a hotel was built on the site of Pidgeon's home for the convenience of packet passengers to Ireland disembarking at the

Martello Tower, Sandymount.

breakwater. In 1814 a military fort was also erected here for the purpose of protecting Dublin port from any possible Napoleonic invasion. The only real employment found for the artillerymen of the Pidgeon House Fort was thirty years later when the guns were pointed menacingly across the bay for the purpose of breaking up the monster Repeal meeting of 1843 which Dan O'Connell had planned to take place at Conquer Hill on the Clontarf Road.

Just before Sandymount DART station can be seen at very close quarters two separate rows of very attractive little dwelling houses — the first a row of sturdy, picturesque stone cottages built in the 1890s by the old DW & WR for some of its rail workers, and the second a row of delightful wooden chalets, like pretty dolls' houses, erected quite recently by the Martin White Community Services for CIE pensioners and their wives.

And just after Sandymount, and before Sydney Parade station, there is a fine view of that interesting gothic church, St John's. Viewed from the DART across the green sward of Monkstown Rugby Club grounds the church is seen at its best on a late summer evening when the warm, sand-coloured stones of its ornamental windows catch the last glows of the western sun. For the opening of this church in 1850 special arrangements were made for trains to stop here, although there were no stations in the immediate vicinity.

The next place of interest after Sydney Parade — and immediately after passing the Coras Trachtala offices (built on the site of a former riding school run by Ireland's foremost lady equestrian, Iris Kellett) — is the 'dramatic' junction of the Strand and Rock Roads, where the old village of Merrion was intersected by the coming of the railway in 1834. I use the word 'dramatic' advisedly; for, after the DART passenger has been gazing out at the continuous stream of city and suburban sights, he or she is plunged with

73

a kind of theatrical and breathtaking suddenness into a panoramic view of the bay. The railway — like a child's eager dash to the water's edge — seems to run almost along the sands and as close to the waves as is prudent. It is a pleasing sight, and one which is difficult to reconcile with the 18th century description of it as one of the most hazardous stretches of coastline near Dublin. Right down to the early years of the last century visible evidence of shipwreck littered Merrion strand. Travellers' accounts, written in the 1800s, refer to the sea at Merrion having numerous hulks and wrecks with their masts peeping ominously above the surface of the water.

In November 1807 occurred one of the greatest sea tragedies on this coast, the loss of the 'Rochdale' and the 'Prince of Wales', both of which set off from the Pidgeon House crammed full of soldiers drawn from the Irish militia and bound for foreign service. A fierce easterly gale accompanied by heavy seas and a blinding snowstorm struck the ships when they were out in the bay and prevented them from either continuing the voyage, beating back to the safety of the port, or putting out anchors. The anchors either dragged or snapped their cables, and the distress flares and signals proved worthless for the storm was such that no rescue boats could get out to the assistance of the ships. Soon night and the swirling snows hid the hapless vessels from view.

Next morning the wreckage of both was found strewn among the rocks and sands from Merrion to Sandycove. Far worse — the drowned, the torn and shattered bodies of crewmen and passengers alike were found in horrifying numbers along the same stretch of coast. Almost 400 people were drowned or dashed to pieces on the sharp rocks; crewmen, soldiers, officers and their families. The only survivors were Captain Jones and the crew of the 'Prince of Wales', together with only four passengers (including a sole woman and child) who had succeeded in escaping with Jones in the ship's longboat. But how had they managed to escape in the height of a storm that had claimed so many lives?

Allegations of dereliction of duty and cowardice came to nought, for the disaster was so complete that the accusers were deprived of any witnesses or eye-witness account regarding the conduct of Jones and his crew. Perhaps the worst postscript to the tragedy was the daylight discovery that from where the 'Rochdale' had struck the rocks a 12-foot gangplank from the ship's quarter-deck could have safely reached the shore — but visibility, down to no more than a few inches in the curtains of swirling snow, must have concealed this fact from the hapless victims.

The coming of the railway, and the raising of Dargan's embankments to carry it, finally obliterated most of the grim reminders of the tragic shipwrecks of the past.

Seapoint/Monkstown

'Monkstown, in the county of Dublin. The Church is a plain stone building, erected in 1797. It belongs to the united parishes of Monkstown, Dalkey, and Killeny. Here is a fine seat, formerly belonging to Lord Ranelagh; also a mansion, which was built on the site of a monastery, whence the name of Monkstown.'

— Leigh's Road-Book of Ireland. 1832

To Seapoint belongs the dubious distinction of having been the location for what was almost certainly the first railway strike in history. In June 1833, eighteen months before the opening of the world's first suburban railway from Westland Row to Kingstown, workmen engaged in constructing the line at Seapoint suddenly downed tools in their pursuance of a claim for a shilling a week increase. For almost two months they'd been working full out, cutting down the seaward face of the cliffs at Salthill, 'pitching' the embankment, building sea walls, and laying the first temporary tracks; and being paid (according to ability) ten, nine or eight shillings for a strenuous 6-day week. But wages weren't always paid regularly every Friday evening, nor were they always paid in 'hard cash'.

The inevitable tiredness and disaffection set in. 'One man called together several of the workmen, and whistling 'Patrick's Day' and the 'Boyne Water' led them through masses of labourers on the shore, encouraging them not to work unless they received higher wages', reported the *Dublin Evening Post*. There was a brief spate of rioting, a call for police reinforcements, the arrest of some of the strike leaders, a week of turmoil in which the strike spread among the 1,500-odd men employed on the entire line. For a few days the prospect of completing the railway looked decidedly grim.

But the strike was poorly organised and without central leadership. Moreover, pressure was brought to bear on the disorganised labourers by local traders who had welcomed the extra money in circulation, and by the clergy reminding their congregations that the rail company was paying higher wages to unskilled labourers than had hitherto been customary in Ireland. After a week without work or wages many of the labourers drifted back to the line and began to take up the recently abandoned wheelbarrows, shovels and picks. The real death blow to the short-lived strike, however, was the decision by William Dargan — the great railway pioneer and builder — to 'pay by results, at $2\frac{1}{2}$d per square foot for the hill work'. The strong and robust men leaped at the chance to add to their weekly earnings by this

75

method, and the less energetic were content to revert to the former system of payment.

The work was quickly resumed, with granite from the Dalkey quarries being brought down 'the metals' by the tramway and then transported by small boats and barges to wherever it was needed along the shoreline from Salthill to Merrion. A further bonus was the timely discovery of a bed of good granite at Seapoint, and much the same at Blackrock, where large quantities of dark limestone — which gave its name to the town — was quarried away for work on the line. The Seapoint granite was used with handsome effect on the construction of a 'tunnel, towers, piers, bridges and bathing places, in the best Italian style and of finely-worked granite' at the point where the railway cut through the grounds of the two most powerful landlords in the area, Lord Cloncurry (Maretimo) and Sir Harcourt Lees (Blackrock House).

Cloncurry's handsome Italiante bridge and twin towers still stand, despite some signs of neglect, a monument not alone to the master stonecutters but also to the persuasive powers of the railway promoters; for it must be mentioned that Cloncurry and Lees — both with land sweeping down to the foreshore — were adamant that they would never permit their magnificent estates to be desecrated by the ugly intrusion of this new-fangled, smoke-belching, noisey, chug-chugging monstrosity! Their adamantine arguments and lordly aloofness were eventually smashed to pieces by the hammer blow of a powerful cash offer: £7,500 to Sir Harcourt Lees and £3,000 to Cloncurry plus the erection of the twin towers and footbridge to give his lordship convenient access to sea bathing and a boating pier. This construction, together with the short tunnel through the small hill forming the boundary of both estates, cost the railway company a whopping £10,000.

Matters didn't end there. Seapoint Avenue had to be moved to make way for the railway 'cutting', while the military insisted on a bridge sturdy enough to withstand heavy artillery being trundled out to the Martello tower. The result? The 'Ordnance Bridge', the only stone overbridge on the original line. And Sir Harcourt, a doughty clergyman who was suddenly converted from implacable foe of rail to ardent champion, now requested a station at Seapoint. He even offered a site, no doubt expecting another handsome cash settlement for his trouble. The company said 'no thanks'.

So residents of Seapoint had to wait more than twenty years before the railway directors obliged them. In 1861 a very narrow site was obtained for a 'moderate price plus season tickets for life for two gentlemen and their wives'. Part of the deal entailed the building of new stables, with little balconies above, to replace some older ones that had been removed. K. A. Murray, in his excellent book *Ireland's First Railway* (published in 1981 by The Irish Railway Record Society, to both of which I am indebted for a great deal of the information contained herein) tells us that 'the building with round windows looking to the railway has mislead many to think that the company had a locomotive shed here'.

Lord Cloncurry's Towers.

Seapoint station is the ideal place from which to set out for a visit to Monkstown Church and the ruins of the old castle about a half mile away. The former is a highly individualistic gothic edifice of the early 19th century, and the latter consists of the remains of a small keep, two-storey gatehouse and part of the curtain wall of a fortification built by the Anglo-Normans to repel the mountain marauders of Gaelic Wicklow.

Monkstown borough also possesses a fine public pavilion, which is a venue for numerous functions and exhibitions throughout the year.

George Russell, AE, (1867-1935), that gifted intellectual — man of letters, artist, theosophist, poet, economist, patriot, and much more besides — once lived at 5 Seapoint Terrace, a few years after his family had quit his birthplace in Co Armagh. He once said: 'I have never been sufficiently grateful to Providence for the mercy shown to me in removing me from Ulster'. A half century later, when he forsook the arid intellectual climate of a new Irish state which he perceived as becoming increasingly confessional, puritanical and repressive of the arts, he may well have thanked the same Providence for removing him from Dublin. He spent the last three years of his life in the more congenial intellectual clime of England.

Salthill

"The lamps at the railroad dotted the line with fire", wrote Thackeray admiringly, as he gazed from the windows of the Salthill Hotel.

The lamps were pretty, from a distance. Close up, they were a 'damn nuisance' according to the enginemen. The same double row of yellow flares found little favour with the locomotive drivers who constantly complained that the large batswing gas burners — more than 200 of them strung out along the entire line — were a 'blinding nuisance' and a hazard. Reluctantly the company had the lamps taken out of service, except at stations and crossings.

And Thackeray, perhaps turning his attention to his fellow-guests in the hotel — and giving rein to his biting humour and merciless observation of human foibles? — may have conceived the idea for *Jeames* and *The Book of Snobs,* the works which established his early reputation when he was groping for a means of expression. In the first he lampoons the new breed of parvenu, the railway speculator: 'Mr Plush, with some hesitation, said he had been speculating in railroads, and stated his winnings to have been thirty thousand pounds. He had commenced his speculations with twenty, borrowed from a fellow-servant.' And James Plush, the footman who quickly becomes 'C. Jeames De La Pluche, Esq.' puts it like this: 'Railway Spec is going on phamusly. You should see how polite they are at my bankers now!'.

Snobs of every ilk — city and military snobs, clerical and literary, political and university, party-going snobs and dining-out snobs, continental, English and Irish snobs — were Thackeray's pet abhorrence and were defined by him as those 'who meanly admire mean things'. Their pretensions, speech and activities were closely pursued and harried:

'The Irish snobbishness develops itself not in pride so much as in servility and mean admirations and trumpery imitations of their neighbours ... Twopenny magnificence, indeed, exists all over Ireland, and may be considered as the great characteristic of the snobbishness of that country ... When Mrs Mulholligan, the grocer's lady, retires to Kingstown, she has 'Mulholliganville' painted over the gate of her villa; and receives you at a door that won't shut, or gazes at you out of a window that is glazed with an old petticoat ... O Ireland! O my country! (for I make little doubt that I am descended from Brian Boru too), when will you acknowledge that two and two make four, and call a pikestaff a pikestaff?'.

Thackeray must have had ample opportunity to observe such types as Jeames and Mrs Mulholligan at the Salthill Hotel. It was the place where the railroad directors and speculators entertained visiting dignitaries, friends of the company, business colleagues and backers, a venue for banquets and board meetings which quickly gained a reputation among the gourmets of Dublin. For the likes of Mrs Mulholligan and her friends there was the amenity of sea-bathing *a la* Brighton. In 1832 Vignoles (one of the railway pioneers) had remarked: 'in no part of the world have I observed so general a taste for bathing as among all classes of society in Dublin and its vicinity ... the establishment of public baths conducted with economy, elegance, and propriety would form a high source of attraction'. So why not build a baths, let it out to a contractor who would undertake to keep the premises in order, provide good towels and bathing dresses, and allow holders of certain rail tickets to bathe at a nominal fee of one penny?

The baths at Salthill were quite elaborate, with two fine stone-lined pools, the larger one for the gentlemen, the smaller one for the ladies, each with enough depth for swimming and with the water renewed with each tide. And in deference to propriety and Victorian modesty there was a high wall between each pool to ensure strict privacy and no 'peeping' and each area had its own bathing boxes and shelters for undressing. There was even stipulations for high walls in front of all the public bathing places along the railway — Salthill, Williamstown, Blackrock etc. — so as to prevent 'such Bathing Places and the Persons bathing therein from being exposed to the View of Passengers on the said Railroad'.

So Mrs Mulholligan could take her dip with an easy mind. But what was the situation when she travelled as a passenger on the train? There was quite a few complaints from outraged passengers who witnessed Dargan's brawny labourers bathing and disporting themselves 'in an indelicate state' during their mealbreak.

In racing against time to build the first railway Dargan had more urgent matters to attend to than the indelicate antics of his workmen. The final section of the original rail line had to be hacked and gouged out of the seaward side of the hill on which stood Salthill House. While his labourers sweated over this task, and then hauled the hacked-out sections of the hill down to fill embankments, Dargan climbed the hill, examined the house, and then decided to rent it. Its suitability was undeniable; it became a kind of operational HQ, with a room set aside in which the directors could confer. As the line approached completion a local caterer, William Marsh, offered the directors £250 per annum in return for permission to run the house as a hotel. Scenting an additional source of revenue, the railway bosses accepted.

The Salthill Hotel was opened to the public on the same day as the railway, December 17, 1834, and that evening the jubilant railway magnates and their friends sat down to a magnificent dinner in Marsh's plush diningroom. It was to be the first of many.

Marsh knew his business. Less than two years later the directors requested their architect, J. S. Mulvaney (who designed the Kingstown station, the pillared entrance to Blackrock station and the impressive 'Gandonian' neo-classical premises of the Royal Irish Yacht Club at Dun Laoghaire) to plan an additional 30 rooms to the hotel. The combination of hotel-station-and-baths enjoyed a 'boom' period of nearly fifty years. But with the existence of the Victoria Baths at the other side of Kingstown the Salthill baths were eventually closed down in the 1880s. The once-fine swimming pools were gradually invaded by the ceaseless tides, and were eventually buried beneath a mound of township waste and refuse. And Salthill House is now demolished.

In 1960 the station — with only a meagre service, and as part of CIE's then policy of giving road transport a greater priority than rail — was closed down.

William Makepeace Thackeray's 'lamps of the railway dotting the line with fire' might have been extinguished for all time but for the introduction of the DART system and the welcomed re-opening of a refurbished station at Salthill in October 1984.

Dun Laoghaire

'Dunleary, or Kingstown, as it is now called in honour of the gracious visit which King George IV was pleased to make to this kingdom, is a convenient harbour, and celebrated sea-bathing village of the county of Dublin. It is well built and extremely agreeable; the Pier adds greatly to its attractions; it divides with Blackrock the favour of the citizens of Dublin as a resort for pleasure parties. A rail-road is about to be established between this place and Dublin. Pop. 1700.'
— Leigh's Road-Book of Ireland. 1832

The railroad was built two years later — and then Dubliners really 'discovered' Dun Laoghaire (or Kingstown, if you prefer).

Not every place in Ireland has a touch of royalty about it. Dun Laoghaire has. It also has that magical quality of appearing to march hand-in-hand with its past. True it is excessively modern in part, but it is also as solid and respectable and as well turned out as a Victorian gent in frock coat, top hat and gold-knobbed cane. Above all it retains a certain 19th century elegance cheek-by-jowl with artisan dwellings, a modern shopping complex, a busy harbour, resort-type hotels and boarding houses, a regal promenade, and quaint side streets. Here and there the stately exclusiveness of some of its tree-lined avenues has all the superiority of a mini-capital city; glimpsed through the iron gates are the dwellings of aristocrats, or, at least, the abodes of merchant princes. You feel, correctly, that levees and 'at homes' were held here, that perhaps tiaras, coronets and ermine-trimmed cloaks might still be found in the attics and cellars of its magnificent houses.

Aye, and that some of its taverns still harbour old salts and hardy seafaring men from the age of sail and the gale-lashed colliers that plied a perilous trade between the harbour and the Welsh ports. Looking at some of them — their huge work-a-day fists dwarfing the pint tulip glasses of jet black-cum-creamy foam — you feel that they may well be the grandsons of smugglers. The lineal descendants of pirates, even? For with all its finery Dun Laoghaire is a lively, accessible, colourful port. Here, at the Victoria Wharf, the Sailors' Reading Room once displayed a notice proclaiming that "... All swearing and improper language, so unbecoming the character of a man, and so dishonouring to God, must be entirely avoided ... Drunkenness, that disgraceful vice which sinks a man below the level of the very beasts that perish, and which is so contrary to order and decency, cannot be permitted an entrance here...". The Sailors' Reading Room is, alas, no more; but the sons of the seafarers are still merrily quaffing and splicing the mainbrace.

Dun Laoghaire owes its special charm not only to its unique location but also to the farsightedness of a couple of early 19th century entrepreneurs, George Smyth and Thomas Gresham. The former, a stone contractor with almost unlimited access to the quarries of fine Dalkey granite with which the harbour was built, erected two imposing neo-classical show houses — 'Stoneview', which became his residence, and 'Granitehall', which he let to wealthy tenants. Thomas Gresham, the Dublin hotelier and one of Dun Laoghaire's foremost developers, built Gresham Terrace and quickly filled the elegant houses with the well-to-do of Dublin city. The sea air was bracing. The boom was on. Thereafter a succession of dignified seafront terraces and hotels sprang up. They were quickly peopled by the Dublin professional classes, the *nouveau riche,* the landed gentry who couldn't quite manage Brighton or Bath, naval officers, retired Indian and Crimean majors — all with their fashionable, marriageable daughters. Kingstown had become the 'in' place.

I would like to have been there on the day they dropped the ancient name Dunleary and — in a flurry of civic self-importance on the occasion of the visit of George IV in 1821! — replaced it with the grandiose appellation Kingstown. A specially erected and brand new royal slipway was hastily built in the inner angle of the East pier to receive his corpulent majesty and entourage. A band, a pavilion, a guard of honour, countless flags and banners and the entire populace were on hand at the appointed hour. Alas, Georgie-Porgy instead turned up, with very little fuss and ceremony, at the rival harbour of Howth beyond Dublin Bay. The Dunlearyites were chagrined. However, all was not lost. After a month-long stay, and wearying of his Irish visit, the jaded voluptuary embarked for home and England from Dunleary, pausing just long enough to mitigate the earlier slight to the red-faced civic dignitaries by allowing them to re-christen their pretty little township Kingstown. Then, without more ado, the Royal paddle-steamer 'Lightning' departed. (In view of the 'now-you-see-me, now-you-don't' royal visit there was an unconscious irony in the ship's name. Perhaps that's why it was subsequently re-named 'Royal Sovereign'?) The paddle-steamer had scarcely disappeared over the horizon when the gleeful civic fathers fell to planning a suitable memorial to commemorate the visit. Within two years the George IV Testimonial Obelisk was erected near the harbour. Fifty years later Thackeray described it as "hideous ... an obelisk stuck on four fat balls and surmounted with a crown on a cushion (the latter were not bad emblems perhaps of the Monarch in whose honour they were raised)."

George IV obelisk, Dun Laoghaire.

81

Dun Laoghaire is full of such stories, still redolent of a rich, glorious, vanished age. Its leisurely and dignified air is best exemplified for me by the famous strike at Downey's pub (a fine red-bricked emporium which, sadly, was demolished some years ago to make way for the present shopping centre). It was the longest strike in history, from 1939 to 1953, and one that was totally lacking in animosity. It was too, like Hegel's definition of the great metaphysical tragedies of our day, not a clash between right and wrong, but rather a clash between right and right — although the original 'rights and wrongs' of the matter are long since lost in the mists of history. But what is still remembered occasionally about the marathon dispute is the urbane, civilized manner in which it was conducted. Throughout the 14-year long 'coolness' the employer and the placard-carrying striker exchanged morning pleasantries and evening salutations. On a wet, cold, miserable day the striker was always invited to leave his placard outside and to come into the warmth of the snug for some 'nourishment'. Lunch hour sandwiches were frequently handed out to him on the pavement and there was always a seasonal gift from the proprietor at Christmas. The striker too was not lacking in courtesy and consideration of the 'boss', and on more than one occasion came to his assistance in the matter of ejecting unruly late night revellers. It was almost a pity that the strike came to an end. It had become a Dun Laoghaire institution. It might easily have become a major tourist attraction.

Dun Laoghaire is pre-eminently a sailor's town, the only Irish port administered directly by the Irish Government and not by a locally-elected board. For more than a century and a half it has been the exit and entry point for the main sea route between Britain and Ireland; it still continues to be the home port of a busy commercial sea fishery, the mail boat terminal, the Sealink car ferry service, the base for Irish Lightships, and one of Ireland's premier yachting centres with the premises of such famous and ancient clubs as the Royal St. George, the Royal Irish, the National and the Dun Laoghaire Motor Yacht Club all more or less cheek-by-jowl on the harbour front. It contains the headquarters of the Irish Yachting Association, the National Sea Training Centre of the Scout Association of Ireland and the National Maritime Museum, the latter housed in what used to be the Mariner's Church.

But for all its salty tang the township doesn't really have a nautical swagger. Architecturally it is unashamedly Victorian — a unique expression of the twin Victorian virtues of business acumen and social respectability. It is surely a gem of its period; its beautiful and impressive Town Hall and Courthouse is an excellent example of the Venetian palazzo style proclaimed by that most eminent of Victorians, John Ruskin; its churches are gothic and Puginesque, their slender spires like gentle, vertical spikes punctuating the predominantly horizontal rows of solid, comfortable, bourgeois terraces. That's the essential Dun Laoghaire, a place that seems always to have been peeking out from behind lace curtains and gazing longingly across the waters to see what its 'betters' were getting up to in Brighton and Bath and Scarborough. Its French renaissance style Royal Marine Hotel of the 1860s was proudly described at the time as 'a first class hotel resembling those which have lately sprung up on the sea-coast of England and on the continent'.

That, I think, says it all.

And that, too, is part of Dun Laoghaire's ineradicable charm.

And the ineradicable charm of Bray now beckons to me. I am anxious to be there. I think I may be permitted to take the DART directly to Bray, for the time being quickly by-passing Sandycove, Glenageary, Dalkey, Killiney and Shankill and postponing the varied delights of those localities until my return journey. Okay?

Dun Laoghaire Town Hall.

Bray

*'Bray is a post town and sea-bathing place of Wicklow, separated from
the county of Dublin by the River Bray, which is famous for its trout.
Here the angler may pass his leisure hours amidst wooded glens and
awful precipices. The vicinity, which is celebrated for its romantic
scenery, abounds with gentlemen's seats. Bray has a neat Church, on an
eminence by the riverside, a R.C. Chapel, a Meeting House, Infantry
Barracks, a Savings Bank, and the remains of an old Castle, near which a
battle took place in 1690, between the forces of James II and William III.*

*About a mile and a half distant is the rocky promontory called Bray
Head, which rises 807 feet above the level of the sea. Its summit may be
reached without much difficulty. The white pebbles found on the shore
beneath it are cut and polished, and are much prized.*

*Pop. 2000. Fairs: May 1 Sept. 20, for cattle and flannels. Inn: Quin's
Hotel.'*

— Leigh's Road-Book of Ireland. 1832

The DART line works up towards Bray as a drama works up towards its
climax. Just as Killiney and Shankill adorn the coast so the massive
promontory of Bray Head, standing high above the sea and the town, crowns
the southern extremity of Dublin Bay. Behind it lies the wild moorlands of
the Wicklow Mountains, below one of Ireland's premier seaside resorts.

Someone once observed that Howth was a seaside place for fishermen,
Dun Laoghaire for gentry, Dalkey for artists, Killiney for lovers — and Bray
a kind of portmanteau to hold the lot. It's true; for Bray is (among other
things) a fishing harbour, a holiday resort, a gateway to the 'Garden of
Ireland', a residential town of handsome urban architecture, an important
shopping area, and was once — perhaps still is, for all I know — the
honeymoon capital of Ireland. It is an undecided hotch-potch of the graceful
and the garish, a conglomerate of elegant Victorian and Edwardian terraces
and squares, lowly cottages and pretty bungalows, restaurants, boarding
houses, hotels and cafes, and a stony beach under a stout sea wall and a broad,
mile-long esplanade. With its ballrooms, discos and fast-food take-aways it is
the nearest thing that Ireland can get to Blackpool, yet its garish lapses are
part and parcel of a town of many charms.

Bray is perhaps too near to Dublin to be considered a part of Co. Wicklow
(which of course it is, and, incidentally, the only part of any other county to
be served by the DART) and perhaps too near the capital to be properly
appreciated by the Dubliner. To some extent it suffers too from the

encroachment of suburbia, but penetrate beyond its neat rows of residential areas and you will find some of the fairest countryside in Leinster. Climb the Head, for example. Even halfway up the path the view of the mountains inland, or the view back towards Killiney, Dalkey Island and across the bay to Howth, is among the most spectacular in Ireland. Or take the narrow cliff walk around the side, or shoulder, of Bray Head, and precipitously high above the single track of the mainline railway. From the cliff walk there are breath-taking views of misshapen crags and coves and rocks carved out by the eternal tides. Flying over the rocks, and with nothing to disturb their solitude, are gulls and fulmars — the latter smaller and distinguishable by their peculiar gliding, stiff-winged flight, and more akin to the albatross than the gull, and quite unknown in Ireland prior to the 1900s. A half hour's stroll along this narrow cliff walk takes one around the Head and to a view southward to Greystones and the eastern coast as far as Wicklow town. But take care, it is not a hike for anyone suffering from vertigo and the Bray Urban District Council have wisely placed notices warning of occasional rock falls!

And nearness to Dublin and the steady drift of Dubliners into his county are gradually killing off the Brayman's 'Wickla' accent, but many of the older folk still cling to a broad pronunciation of words which is quite unlike the Dublin version. Generations of resistance to the incursions of the sea and the harsh hilly life have bred sturdily independent men and women and left a stubborn streak in the Wicklow character. It used to be said that you had to know Wicklow people well before you liked them and even longer before they liked you. What you don't recognise at first is that while their slightly taciturn exterior is carefully cultivated, the warmth of their hearts is perfectly natural.

desmondmurphy · 85

IRISH ENGINEERING DUBLIN SEVILLE WORKS 1853

Which, apart from the undeniable scenic attractions of the place, may account for its popularity. And that popularity began with the coming of the railway. At Bray's DART station can be seen the original iron pillers — still happily in use and supporting the platform roof — and bearing the legend 'Irish Engineering Co., Seville Works, 1853'. Before that date Bray was nothing more than a quiet market village with a main street and a few cottages on the strand. From the mid-1850s onwards it quickly blossomed into a busy and handsome resort. Everybody who was anybody came to it at one time or another. Writers especially seemed to have found something both salutary and inspiring in its bracing sea air — the famous, like Sir Arthur Conan Doyle (creator of the world's most famous detective, Sherlock Holmes) who once lived at Raheen; Oscar Wilde, at Tower Cottage; and even the less famous such as James Murphy, once a schoolteacher in Bray and who wrote many historical romances, the most notable being *The Shan Van Vocht* (1883) and Ella MacMahon, a clergyman's daughter who produced more than twenty 'formula' novels of workingclass seduction, with the 'fate worse than death' usually taking place on a Bank Holiday excursion to Bray. Like so many places on the DART line Bray too has its Joycean connection.

I sometimes wonder if Joyce's father would have welcomed the introduction of the DART system? I'm inclined to doubt it. It was to 1 Martello Terrace, Bray, that Joyce *pére* moved with his wife and young family in September 1887, not only for the healthy sea air but also to be removed from his in-laws. 'The train fare would keep them away' John Joyce explained. Today's relatively cheap DART fares, with a seven-day service from early morning until late at night, would have enabled his in-laws to catch up on him! And yet, conversely, what a boon the DART would have been to the elder Joyce as he flitted from one address to another — Sandymount, Blackrock, Bray etc. — constantly uprooting his family in a vain endeavour to dodge his creditors and his in-laws.

The house at Martello Terrace is still there, still largely unchanged, with the first floor drawing room where the Joyces and their Sunday visitors gathered round the piano with their drinks and songs, the dining room which was the scene of the Christmas dinner scene in *A Portrait of the Artist as a Young Man*. The room contains the fireplace where 'Mr Dedalus looked at himself in the pierglass above the mantelpiece, waxed out his moustache ends and then, parting his coat-tails, stood with his back to the glowing fire'.

Bray, no less than Dun Laoghaire and Blackrock, has retained much of its Victorian character. Along with its grand seafront terraces it has the usual medium-sized two-storeyed dwellings with bay windows and the columnar door frames which were intended to evoke the sort of Georgian grandeur so beloved of their middleclass occupants. For Bray came into being when the emerging Catholic bourgeois — the Castle Catholics — and their Protestant neighbours were beginning to find easy accommodation each with the other. Something of that easy accommodation is evident in the wit of Fr. Healy, the almost legendary parish priest of Bray, who delighted in exchanging quips with his Protestant friends, the vicar of Dalkey and the rector of Bray. When the latter once remarked to Fr Healy that he had been sixty years in the world and had yet to discover the difference between a good Catholic and a good Protestant, the priest replied: 'You won't be sixty seconds in the next world until you find out', to which came the instant and smiling rejoinder: 'Yes, I would prefer Heaven for climate but Hell for society as all my friends are Catholics'.

And on a note of merry repartee I propose to bid adieu to Bray, a seaside resort for all tastes, for there is little about entertaining family parties and excursionists and retired colonels and genteel dowagers that it does not know.

Bray to Howth

Killiney

'Killeny Hill is 8 miles from Dublin. On its summit is a conspicuous obelisk, whence the traveller may enjoy a rich reward for his toil in ascending the mountain, in the diversified prospects of sea and land which the situation commands.'

— Leigh's Road-Book of Ireland. 1832

If the DART day tripper decided to select only one station as a disembarkation point for an exploratory outing into the 'sprawling museum' of Co. Dublin then he or she could do no better than to get off at Killiney. By climbing the steep lane almost directly opposite the station — a steady ten minute walk at most — one comes across the well-preserved ruins of an early Christian church. A 6th century chieftain of the locality, Leinin, is credited with the building of the church for his five daughters, all of whom were nuns, and thus giving a name to one of the most beautiful districts in the Dublin DART area — Cill Inghiann (the church of the daughters) or Cill Leinin (the church of Leinin) and hence Killiney.

There is a charm attached to old churches leaning their shattered naves in green nettles. Ireland is studded with them. Leinin's chapel is still in fairly good condition, a fine example of early Irish Christian architecture and yet oddly incongruous above a shoreline which seems a curious compromise between the Emerald Isle and Italy. If the day tripper should doubt this then I suggest turning away from the ancient church stones and, scarcely a dozen paces away, peering through the gateway of a house called Campanella and looking across its glorious garden down towards Killiney strand and the Black Castle and the White Rock bathing place. There I rest my case.

However, if the tripper is not overly interested in ancient churches then I suggest visiting or viewing the fairytale extravaganza of the Killiney Court Hotel, which is even closer to the station. Its lounge contains old railway memorabilia in the form of attractively framed prints and newspaper accounts, and the original house, Cuirt-na-Farraga (around which part of the modern hotel has not unsympathetically formed itself) stands as a kind of memorial to that much-maligned figure of fiction, the Victorian nanny or governess.

Fulmar, Killiney Bay.

Who was she, this faithful and almost forgotten family retainer who so loved her little charges, the Exham children, that when her time came to be pensioned off she pleaded to be allowed to remain with them? We don't know her name; we suspect a gentle, perhaps lonely, person without kinfolk of her own. All we do know is that she readily offered to the Exham family the legacy that had come to her too late in life to be enjoyed in return for being allowed to remain in the family service. When she died the Exhams used the proceeds of the nanny's legacy to build Cuirt-na-Farraga, the sea court. The instinct of a fiction writer suggests to me that there is a gothic romance hidden somewhere in the origins of Killiney Court Hotel.

And the same instinct tells me that there is a great romance lost in the half-tale of poor Etty Scott and her dreams of buried treasure on Killiney Hill. Etty was the daughter of one of the quarriers who had helped to gouge out the rock for the building of Dun Laoghaire harbour. By the late 1820s the work was completed, the bulk of the quarry face exposed, and the miners and quarrymen were being laid off. The bonanza days were over for the stone workers. Or were they? No, not quite, for one night Etty had a vivid dream in which she saw a hoard of Viking gold hidden among the rocks somewhere on Dalkey Common. She told her father of the dream, even described the location. At first he was sceptical. When Etty's dream recurred on succeeding nights he began to search and to dig. Some of his mates joined in. Just when the treasure seekers were beginning to attract notice — and no end of jibes! — a stone coffin containing Saxon and Danish coins was accidentally discovered in the grounds of an old coaching inn which stood on the site of the present Killiney House. The great Dalkey gold rush was on with a vengeance!

For days and nights gangs of unemployed quarrymen toiled relentlessly all over the twin hills of Dalkey and Killiney. Etty's nocturnal visions kept pace with their frenzied searching, spurring them on. Each dream revealed a new location. Outsiders, attracted by the gold fever, swarmed into the area. Massive rocks were overturned and hacked and gouged with a greater energy than had ever been employed in quarrying for harbour stone. But nothing was found. Inevitably there were mutterings and the beginning of whisperings that Etty Scott might be imagining things; worse, that she might be a witch and in league with dark forces. One night the startled gold hunters dropped their picks and shovels and raced in terror from a hillside that had suddenly become alive with the most horrendous shrieks and the fearful threshing and flailing and ghostly lights of demonic creatures in the brush. It was later discovered to be nothing more sinister than a cruel practical joke perpetrated by some tipsy students. The pranksters had callously tied two cats by their tails, painted them with phosphorus, and then let them loose on the hillside. The ridicule provoked by the incident put an end to the gold hunt. Poor Etty Scott with her dreams and visions retreated into that oblivion reserved for nine day wonders.

The only gold on Killiney Hill is that of samphire and gorse and yellow vetch, its greatest treasure that of breathtaking views of the bay below and Bray Head and the Wicklow mountains. There are scenes here to delight the eye of a Paul Henry or a Turner and to make poets write reams of inspired verse.

A good route for the walker is to follow Station Road, parallel to the DART line and the strand, to Victoria Road and Killiney village; from there, opposite the Druid's Chair pub, to ascend the hill to the obelisk which surmounts it and which affords the most exquisite views. The obelisk contains a plaque which reads: 'Last year being hard with the poor, the walks about these hills and this obelisk were erected by John Mapas. June 1742'. Colonel Mapas had built Killiney House two years before, and the obelisk and hill walks were intended to provide much-needed work for the local unemployed. Close by the obelisk is a wishing stone curio. Legend has it that if you walk around each level, from base to top, your wish will come true. Don't waste your time wishing for some of Etty Scott's hidden gold, but your wish will be instantly granted if you desire nothing more than exquisite views of sea birds wheeling over the endless tides of the crescent-shaped bay below, the woods of Ayesha Castle stretching down to the road and in Springtime delighting the eye with primroses and bluebells. The gothic arch which spans the road below was once the original entrance to Ayesha; the delightful ribbon of the Vico Road — the coastal link between Killiney and Dalkey — was opened in June 1889 by the Lord Lieutenant and Marchioness of Londonderry. That road, and some of the little stone alleys leading down from the Hill Road to the beach put me in mind of similar stone *vicoli* at Nesso and Torno plunging down to Lake Como. Little wonder then that while I can admire so many places around Dublin I can love Killiney.

The walker should continue the short distance from Killiney Hill to its neighbour Dalkey Hill, to which it is connected by a saddleback ridge. Both hilltops are laid out as a public park, complete with nature trail, the remains of an ancient church and the collection of stones known as the 'Druid's Chair'. From Dalkey Hill — with its magnificent panorama of the wide loop of the Liffey valley, the city, Howth, the heaving waters of Dublin Bay and the distant Cooley peninsula beyond Dundalk — via Cunningham Road one can descend again to the Dalkey DART station, in all a hike of no more than two hours from Killiney station if one doesn't linger too long over the views.

Obelisk, Killiney Hill.

91

Dalkey

'Dalkey, in Dublin, is a beautiful village, celebrated for its ancient castles, the remains of two of which are still standing. On Dalkey Hill is a cromlech, and on the Common are remains of a Druidical circle. Immediately above the village rises a mountain, and before it is a sound, or channel, with sufficient water for ships of burden, separating it from Dalkey Island. On this island, which consists of about eighteen acres of sweet herbage, may be seen a Martello Tower, and a church in ruins. Here, as in many parts of Ireland, the people elect a king from among themselves, to whom, occasionally, they pay certain tributes. Pop. 760.'

— Leigh's Road-Book of Ireland. 1832

"I am a product of Dalkey's outlook", George Bernard Shaw once wrote to a friend.

That great Shavian scholar and Dublin historian, John O'Donovan, tells us that in his old age Shaw was fond of repeating that the happiest moment of his life was when, at ten years of age, his mother told him that they were going to live in a little six-room cottage on Torca Hill in Dalkey.

For the ten-year-old boy it meant an escape from Dublin — he was always to retain a certain contempt for the city's less attractive aspects — and it meant the freedom to roam freely about a scenic hilltop overlooking the splendid sweep of Dublin Bay; it meant climbing the hill to the cromlech, visiting the old castle, bathing at the White Rock below the Common, and "best of all, no Sunday church. The family gave up church-going when they went to Dalkey and did not resume it on returning to Hatch Street."

Perhaps Dalkey also meant an escape from the prying and curious neighbours in Hatch Street. For the Shaw family were 'odd' enough to invite prurient gossip: the husband was a drunkard of shabby genteel background and snobbish inclinations; the wife was an amateur prima donna who seemed so inordinately attached to her colourful and attractive singing teacher, John Vandeleur Lee, as to gladly allow him to set up a joint household with the Shaws in No 1 Hatch Street. And it was the bachelor Lee who provided the holiday home at Dalkey, where, presumably, the strange *ménage a trois* could establish itself more openly.

At any event everyone seemed quite happy at Dalkey during those summers of the late 1860s — Shaw senior (no doubt with his jar by his side) had the status of both a town address and a holiday home which he could never have afforded from his own means alone; Mrs Shaw was living with all the semblance of respectability under the same roof as the man who had displaced her husband in her affections; the son George was happily roaming about at will; the two teenage daughters, Lucy and Elinor, were receiving musical instruction from the charming Vandeleur Lee; and the latter was taking more than a musical interest in the lovely Lucy.

It couldn't go on. Time, and the more prosaic surroundings of Hatch Street, wrought change. In 1873 Mr Shaw — suddenly converted to teetotalism — considered initiating legal proceedings over the relationship between his wife and Lee. While he was dithering, Lee on the other hand was running foul of Dublin's most influential musicians. A musical innovator and the inventor of a 'new method of voice training' Lee's technical deficiencies were mercilessly exposed by Sir Robert Stewart, Professor of Music at Trinity College, and Dublin's foremost musical authority. Lee, humiliated, fled to London. Within weeks Mrs Shaw and her two daughters followed him, though not before she had sold all the Hatch Street furniture and bric-a-brac and fixed up her husband and son in comfortable 'bachelor' lodgings.

Three years later, with his father dead and buried, the 20-year-old George Bernard packed a portmanteau and quit Dublin forever. The only truly happy and abiding memories he took with him were of boyhood summers in Dalkey . . . .

What then is this 'Dalkey outlook'? Like all attempts to define something, or some place, of infinite charm it is well nigh impossible to answer the question. Where Dun Laoghaire may be said to possess a touch of royalty, Dalkey (notwithstanding its annual and centuries-old custom of electing a 'king' from among the citizens) may be said to possess a touch of the Mediterranean. From the hill top, on a bright summer day, the view of the bay and the gentle curve of Killiney strand is said by many to rival the glories of Naples and Sorrento. It is no idle boast. Some, in fact, would claim that Dublin Bay is a gentler, prettier, more perfect crescent than its more famous rival. The blue of the sea is no less brilliant, the green of hilltop and mountain slope and distant fields considerably more verdant. Below the town there are deep, sea-weedy pools among the rocks in which youngsters may spend many sunny hours netting 'tiddlers' or searching for crabs. The stretch of beach at Killiney has become to generations of lucky children a very heaven. Across these sands and loose shingle of tiny pebbles they gallop ponies, run races, build castles, play ball and rush out into the plashy semi-circle of wavelets. With the sea on two sides of Dalkey you are seldom far from the sight of it, the sound of it or the magic of it.

The dread history of it too. Throughout the Middle Ages and right down to the 16th century Dalkey, and not Dun Laoghaire, was the principal port to the south of Dublin city. It was part of a grim coastline when the gale was in full force and you can still see what a heavy toll was levied by the storms on the fishermen and foreign sailors alike if you visit Dalkey churchyard. A tombstone there records the fact that 380 people lost their lives in a

November gale of 1807 in which two ships were wrecked to pieces on the nearby coast. This and succeeding disasters, and the immense waste of life and property each year, resulted in the drawing up of a petition calling for the provision of an 'asylum' harbour in Dublin Bay. The granite of Dalkey quarry went to the building of such harbours at Dun Laoghaire and Howth. The first lifeboats in Ireland — propelled by powerful and brave oarsmen — put out regularly from the slipways of Dalkey and Dun Laoghaire in the height of the storms. The heroic Captain Boyd and the Dun Laoghaire Harbour Master, Hutchinson, were among the many who perished in rescue attempts.

But, forbidding as some aspects of Dalkey's maritime history may be, few fail to fall under the spell of the place. You visit it for its variety — its 'villagey' character side-by-side with the sophistication and elegance of its sister township, Dun Laoghaire. It yields nothing in grace and charm to the larger borough, yet there is a solidity about the place that is very satisfying. Its crowning glory is colour — the mica of granite sparkling in sunlight, the green and brown of bracken, the gold of gorse, the clear blue of the sea below, and the deep, dim blue of the Hill of Howth across the water.

Dalkey is also a place of old weathered stones — like the stones of Archibold's Castle, a reminder that Dalkey was once a walled medieval town intended to persuade the hardy O'Toole and O'Byrne clansmen outside that the garrison inside was stronger in numbers than it really was. Across the street from Archibold's Castle is a 16th century castellated stone house which has been restored and is now the Town Hall. Then there are the ancient and picturesque stones of St Begnet's Church on Dalkey Island, an example of the early Irish style of ecclesiastical architecture, plus the stones of the island's Martello Tower and the massive shards of granite that hem in and seem to dwarf tiny Coliemore Harbour, and the stones of neighbouring Bulloch Harbour and Castle.

In the Middle Ages the pretty little anchorage of Bulloch was a walled-in, heavily-fortified, self-contained settlement under the control of the Cistercian monks of St Mary's Abbey, Dublin. In the palmy days of Bulloch's quasi independence the abbot was practically an uncrowned king for he had the monopoly on all goods for transhipment through the harbour and

Dalkey Island.

94

overland to Dublin — and he had a rake-off from all wrecks on the coast! The fortified walls, however, were of scant use to the 60-odd inhabitants of the place when the Cromwellian Colonel Craford lead a party of his roundhead raiders into Bulloch in 1641. The hapless villagers, already terrified by rumours of Cromwellian atrocities at Clontarf across the bay, immediately took to their boats. Craford pursued them. When he quickly overtook them he ordered his men not to waste musket ball and powder but to toss every man, woman and child overboard. All were tragically drowned.

Small boats are available at Bulloch and Coliemore for the sea angler. Off Dalkey Island and the Muglins (where, at one time, the bodies of pirates hung in chains and clanked their ominous warning to other nautical lawbreakers) there is fishing for coalfish, pollack, tope, skate and conger. Out further, on the Burford and Kish banks, blonde and thornback ray, turbot and brill, plaice and dab are among the more common species taken on the hook. In fact the whole coastal area from Dun Laoghaire (where fishing from the rocks and piers is popular, and free) to Killiney strand (where boats for hire are also to be had) abounds in bass, flounder, codling and sea trout.

And something in this indefinable 'Dalkey outlook' must operate wonderfully to inspire prolific playwrights, plants and painters. In addition to Shaw it seems to have helped foster the dramatic talents and play writing skills of Hugh Leonard and Lennox Robinson (1886-1958). Robinson has been described by author John Cowell as 'the most prolific playwright ever found by the Abbey Theatre' and when Robinson purchased Sorrento Cottage on Dalkey's famed Vico Road in 1925 he soon set about staging open air productions of Greek plays in Sorrento's terraced gardens. Fifty years before Robinson a previous owner of the cottage, Sir Francis Brady, was responsible for another curious production — the indigenous floral rarity *senecio cineraria maritima,* or Dalkey Ragwort. Among the 400 different species of flora that grow so abundantly in the Dalkey/Killiney region this ragwort must surely be the one with the greatest claim to be considered as the floral emblem of the district. It originated in a packet of seed sown by Sir Francis in his Sorrento Cottage garden in 1875, from whence it quickly escaped, then quickly hybridised with common ragwort — and has been quickly spreading ever since.

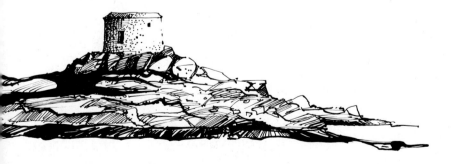

And after playwrights and plants, painters. With good reason there are a number of artists' studios in the Dalkey neighbourhood. While the playwright and poet may prefer solitude for their writings, painters are somewhat like starlings. They seem to work and paint better in colonies. Is this so that they may be better able to borrow brushes and tubes of colour from each other? And what do they paint? Dalkey mainly ... which is a fisherman mending nets at his leisure, and red-sailed boats riding at anchor in the little harbours, and the bluey-green sea, and old castles, and quaint streets and houses and cottages and gardens radiant with sunflowers, geraniums, fuschia and hollyhocks.

Like George Bernard Shaw, their multifarious canvasses are products of Dalkey's outlook.

Glenageary/'Atmospheric' Rail

The rail line from Dalkey to Dun Laoghaire (via Glenageary and Sandycove stations) is not much over 3,000 yards in length. As such it scarcely merits a faint pen squiggle on any map of European rail development; and yet it exists today as a kind of curious memorial to one of the greatest rail experiments of all time — the first-ever 'Atmospheric Railroad'. Though for the most part hemmed in by coursed granite rubble supporting lofty walls, the line is a reminder to the commuter, the railroad buff and the historian of one of the glorious failures of 19th century technology.

The 1830s was a decade of invention, innovation and entreprenurial speculation. Particularly where rail and steam were involved. The Irish rail magnates — James Pim, C. B. Vignoles and their associates — flushed with the unqualified success of having given Ireland its first steam railroad, now cast about for more worthy and profit-making achievements. An extension to Dalkey was envisaged. And now, almost on the heels of their steam locomotive triumph the directors of the Dublin to Kingstown Railway were hearing strange reports of a new invention — a railway run entirely on air! Inventor Sam Clegg was rumoured to be conducting experiments in London on an 'atmospheric railroad'.

Clegg was working on an intricate, but revolutionary, system — basically a length of tube fixed centrally between the rails, with a projecting arm from the underside of the lead carriage which passed down into the tube and supported a long rod, to the forward end of which was affixed a piston, and to the rear, a balancing counterweight. Leather cup-rings made the piston airtight. When air was pumped out of the main pipe the vacuum sucked the piston along.

With the aid of the Samuda ship building firm on the Thames Clegg had made a few trial runs in London with a view to having his invention adopted by the new rail companies. The Dublin and Kingstown directors sent their man, James Pim, over to have a look. Pim liked what he saw, and as Clegg's system required a 'proper' trial ground for more extensive testing, Pim eagerly suggested the largely disused tramway (the 'Metals') which had until recently conveyed stone from the Dalkey quarries to Kingstown for harbour building. It was eminently suitable and the gradients would give Clegg's invention a real chance of showing its capabilities. Clegg and the Samuda brothers jumped at the chance.

Work began in September 1842, William Dargan once more receiving the construction contract. A continuous cast-iron tube was laid from Dalkey to Dun Laoghaire along the centre line between the rails. The terminus, at Barnhill Road, had a pumping house with three boilers. Trials now began. At a given signal the pump house evacuated the air from the tube. Air pressure then propelled the pistons (connected to the lead carriage by the projecting arm) along the tube, drawing the train with it. Elaborate precautions were taken to ensure that the tube would reseal after the train passed over. Leather flap-valves, which opened and closed again as the rod passed along, were greased with a composition of wax and tallow and the underside of the train was fitted with a kind of giant clothes iron. This was filled with burning charcoal and, as the train moved along the rails, the iron pressed the leather, closing it and re-melting the wax and forming a seal.

During the tests a train of nearly 65 tons got up to Dalkey from Kingstown in less than four minutes. Speeds of up to 40 mph were recorded. The return journey was by gravity, with the piston and its attachments drawn up to one side to clear the main pipe, and the train starting its descent when the brake was released on the first carriage. The Victorian engineering world was agog with excitement at this new method of propulsion. While tests were in progress scientists and engineers were welcomed to inspect the Atmospheric and conduct their own trials and experiments. Austria, France, Belgium and Germany sent over their best men to seek information. The French representative, Mallet, in an exhaustive report recommended the system for the French railways and mentioned a speed of 70 mph as having been achieved on the line. A scientist named Elrington was experimenting with the equipment; through an oversight the piston carriage had not been coupled to the train, and the 'start' signal was given. The piston carriage shot off on its own — hitting a top speed of 85 mph and completing the journey from Kingstown to Dalkey in less than two minutes! But for the quick action of the astonished crew and their strenuous exertions on the brake, the piston carriage, and all on board her, would have smashed into the Dalkey dead-end. Despite this near disaster — or perhaps because of it? — the accelerative power of the Atmospheric was much vaunted and admired. So too was its cleanliness. Noise, showers of cinders, clouds of smoke and vapour, were all part and parcel of rail travel in the early years. But the Atmospheric did away with all that unpleasantness. One user wrote: '... the travelling was most luxurious; no noise, no smoke, no cinders, no smell'. Little wonder then that no less an expert than the great Victorian engineer, I. K. Brunel (who built the tunnel at Sorrento, Dalkey, in 1847) convinced his fellow directors of Britain's Great Western Railway that they should adopt the Atmospheric for their South Devon railway.

Why then was the system dubbed a 'glorious failure'? The short answer is 'rats'. Though the 'Atmospheric' worked satisfactorily for eleven years, 1843-1854, and provided the only means of rail transport between Dalkey and Kingstown, where passengers changed to the parent line, it had been a costly experiment. The biggest difficulty lay in the working of the leather valving system. Every time a train passed over, it treated the leather quite brutally and the 'clothes iron' device didn't do an effective job of re-sealing the flaps. The cost of repairing and replacing them proved much greater than at first anticipated. Ultimately the company had to employ a number of 'valve' men to follow each train on foot and press down the leather flaps. But what no one had reckoned on was the hordes of rats nightly attracted to a palatable diet of the tallow-soaked leather. They persistently gorged themselves on the valve flaps. It could even be said that they gnawed the noble 'Atmospheric' experiment to a standstill.

And from the ridiculousness of a swarm of ravenous rats to the sublime sadness of a poet's epitaph....

It was from his home in Glenageary in December 1908 that the poet and playwright John Millington Synge sent a little collection of poems to Yeats at the Cuala Press, Dundrum. One of the poems, entitled 'On An Anniversary', contained the lines:

And so when all my little work is done
They'll say I came in Eighteen-seventy-one,
And died in Dublin . . . What year will they write
For my poor passage to the stall of Night?

Synge died three months later, on March 24th 1909, while the little book of *Poems and Translations* was still passing through the press. Yeats (who described his friend Synge as 'a solitary, undemonstrative man, never asking pity, nor complaining, nor seeking sympathy') enquired of one of the nurses in the hospital where Synge died if the playwright knew he was dying; the nurse replied: 'He may have known it for months but he would not have spoken of it to anyone'.

In fact Synge knew some twelve months before that he was dying, though he told no one about it but his fiancee, the Abbey actress Maire O'Neill. In September 1909, when submitting his poems to Yeats for publication, Synge had said of them: 'I do not feel very sure of them; yet enough of myself has gone into them to make me sorry to destroy them, and I feel at times it would be better to print them while I am alive than to leave them after me to go God knows where'.

The poems were published fifteen days after his death.

Sandycove

The station-master, noticing our camera and notebooks, immediately sensed the purpose of our mission: "The Martello Tower? Just turn right on leaving the station, then first left. You can't miss it as soon as you come in sight of the sea. About fifteen minutes walk."

We thanked him. Outside, my wife Mary said: "Obviously directions to the tower must be the most frequent request from tourists and visitors to Sandycove".

I agreed. But why should a squat, rotund tower that has been described as something between a 'foreshortened butter churn and a gigantic brick-built pressure cooker' have become a mecca for tourists and worldwide literati?

Tall, stately and elegant round towers we can understand. Like celtic crosses and fairy mounds they are emblematic of Ireland, all rooted in a misty Gaelic past. But a bluff, blunt, squat military fortification (modelled, and hence named, after a defensive tower at Cape Mortello in Corsica, and built in 1804 to withstand the Napoleonic invasion that never materialised) — why should such a building excite so much interest?

Well, for one thing it commands vistas that have made the location scenically famous — the superb crescent of Dublin Bay, with the Hill of Howth away off northwards, the spires and steeples of the city shimmering in the haze of morning light, the sea and the Muglin Rocks and Dalkey Island, the Dublin foothills and the Wicklow mountains inland and to the south-west, with wispy tresses of grey mist stealing quietly down their great dark shoulders. And for another thing — for some, the most important thing! — James Joyce used the Sandycove Martello Tower as the starting place for the most important day in modern literature, Bloomsday, 16 June 1904.

Nobody who has read *Ulysses* can glimpse or pass the tower without visualizing 'stately plump Buck Mulligan' in his yellow ungirdled dressing gown lifting his shaving mug to the morning sun.

Buck Mulligan, of course, was the real life Oliver St John Gogarty who had rented the tower from the British Secretary of State for War at a sum of £8 yearly. He had a notion — some might say a grandiose vision — of establishing the tower as a kind of new Delphi, with himself as the oracle and a few younger and lesser poets as his acolytes. Joyce and another paying guest, Samuel Chenevix Trench (the Englishman 'Haines' in *Ulysses*) joined Gogarty there. Joyce departed after a week, regarding himself as having been evicted — driven out by a build up of tension, Trench's nightmares involving a black panther and Gogarty's dramatic remedy for such nightmares, namely, discharging a revolver in the dark and aiming it at a collection of pans on the shelf above Joyce's head. Joyce left in a huff, in the middle of the night, and avenged himself much later by mercilessly portraying Gogarty as the flippant Buck Mulligan in his masterpiece.

History was to add another twist of vengeance. Gogarty, still grooming the bizarre 'gentleman's residence' of the Martello Tower to be his own future memorial, wrote the following jesting words to his erstwhile friend Joyce in 1908: '...Is there any reason why your ashplant shall not be made the centre of the collection in the 'National Joyce Museum, Cabra?' ...'

The jest back-fired, as jests so often do in Ireland. Today Joyce's elegant walking cane (while not the actual ashplant referred to in Gogarty's letter, nor the centrepiece of Sandycove's collection of Joyceana) is nonetheless prominently displayed in the Martello Tower which, since 1962, has housed the Joyce Museum and has become internationally known as 'Joyce's Tower'. Meanwhile, try asking the average Dubliner for directions to 'Gogarty's Tower' — nine times out of ten you'll get either a blank expression, a shrug, a quizzical stare, or a short pithy phrase containing a certain four-letter word with which the average Dubliner cloaks his ignorance or expresses his contempt. Enough said.

And today the ever-growing collection of Joycean memorabilia at the tower — manuscripts, letters, rare and early editions of the author's work, paintings, photos, his guitar, piano, his waistcoat and tie, etcetera — are viewed by thousands of visitors each summer. While the chief exhibit is undoubtedly the tower itself, with its walls of eight-foot thick Wicklow granite and its sweeping view of Dublin Bay, I personally prefer the exhibit referred to in the following words of the Museum's curator Robert Nicholson: "Of all the portraits of Joyce in the Tower, the most absorbing is his own face, cast in bronze after his death. On the lips of the death-mask is a curious, contented half-smile — as if he was still chuckling over the trick he had played on Gogarty."

Sandycove has other literary associations — Shaw, L.A.G. Strong, Monk Gibbon, Padraic Colum. The latter's father was once the station master here. Earlier he had been the workhouse superintendent at Longford, where the future poet was born in 1882, the eldest of seven children. When the elder Colum obtained more congenial employment at Sandycove he moved with his family to the railway cottage at Eden Road, Glasthule. From there the young Padraic attended the local national school before gaining a railway clerkship and then embarking on his long and distinguished career as playwright and poet.

George Bernard Shaw once attended a private school run by William Halpin in Lawson Terrace, only a few hundred yards from the Joyce Tower. Another resident of Lawson Terrace was Sir Roger Casement, who was born at number 29 in September 1864. The house, originally called Doyle's Cottage, was later divided into two separate abodes, each of which share a central plaque commemorating the executed patriot who was hanged as a

Note: The Joyce Tower is open to the public every day from May to September, and may be viewed by appointment during the rest of the year by telephoning the Curator.

'traitor' at Pentonville Prison on August 3, 1916, making him the 'sixteenth' of the Easter Rebellion martyrs immortalised in the poem *Sixteen Dead Men*. Casement's conviction and subsequent execution was to some extent engineered by showing copies of his 'black diaries' to various influential people at the time of his trial, thus counteracting the widespread sympathy for his tragic position engendered by his many British and American friends. The notorious diaries, which many believe to be an ignoble and wretched forgery, not only besmirched Casement's reputation as a high-minded patriot and as a humane opponent of all injustice, but also helped to sign his death warrant.

Wretched forgeries provide a link with another former resident of Sandycove, the venal and meanly ambitious journalist Richard Pigott. As a young man ever on the lookout for anything that might further his self-advancement (and hacking out a tawdry livelihood on the fringes of the newspaper and legal professions) Pigott had a brief and minor run-in with an apprentice solicitor in Newry named Charles Russell. Forty years later, in February 1889, they were to meet each other again in the highly-charged atmosphere of the Old Bailey courthouse, London. The occasion was the investigation by a commission of judges into the authenticity of letters which charged Parnell and others with conspiracy and which seemed to prove the Irish leader's complicity in crime, specifically the Phoenix Park murders. The serious point in the charges was the publication by *The Times* of letters in facsimile purporting to have been written by Parnell. The first letter ran:

Dear Sir — I am not surprised at your friend's anger but he and you should know that to denounce the murders was the only course open to us ... But you can tell him and all others concerned that though I regret the accident of Lord F. Cavendish's death I cannot refuse to admit that Burke got no more than his deserts.

You are at liberty to show him this and others whom you can trust but let not my address be known. He can write to the House of Commons.

Yours very truly,
Chas S. Parnell.

The second letter was even more damning and looked like clear evidence of actual instigation and incitement to murder. It ran as follows:

What are these people waiting for? This inaction is inexcuseable. Our best men are in prison and nothing is being done. Let there be an end to this hesitancy. Prompt action is called for. You promised to make it hot for old Forster and Co. Let us have evidence of your power to do so....

Yours very truly,
Chas S. Parnell.

Not only Parnell — who vehemently denounced the letters as 'villainous and bare-faced' forgeries — but the entire Irish nationalist movement was on trial. And the former Newry solicitor Charles Russell (now a knighted QC and one of the luminaries of the English Bar) was there to defend Parnell and Irish constitutionalism. Opposite him, in the witness box, sat the perennially hard-up and hitherto unknown hack journalist Richard Pigott. The case hinged on the authenticity of the letters. It was not contended by *The Times* that the body of either letter was in Parnell's actual handwriting, only the signature. (Prior to the widespread use of the typewriter it was customary for a secretary to provide the body of a letter, the principal adding his signature at the bottom.)

Sir Charles Russell, a man of marvellous physical and mental vigour, excelled in courtroom cross-examination. It was by forceful questioning rather than by subtlety that he extracted the truth. In the middle of a relentless and incisive cross-examination he suddenly requested Pigott to write down a list of random words. The hapless Pigott seized on the respite thus offered and quickly jotted down the words as Sir Charles called them out. Pigott's list contained the two curious misspellings of the words 'inexcuseable' and 'hesitancy' which coincided with those in the letters. Under further merciless questioning he quickly broke down and confessed to having forged the letters.

Parnell, vindicated, received a standing ovation when he entered the House of Commons that evening. Pigott, ruined and discredited, and now facing possible charges of forgery and perjury, was already on the boat train to France. A few days later he blew his brains out in a shabby hotel room in Madrid.

Sandycove is a popular place for wind-surfing and canoeing and in Scotsman's Bay (immediately outside Dun Laoghaire's east pier and sweeping round to meet Joyce's tower and the 'Forty Foot') water-skiing also is a frequent pastime. On most summer weekends teams of wind-surfers, canoeists and skiiers can be seen displaying their skills. And all year round, summer and winter, there are frequent acquatic 'displays' of another sort at the renowned 'Forty Foot' bathing place, a secluded and picturesque seawater retreat for hardy swimmers. The scene of a traditional Christmas Day plunge for over a century, the 'Forty Foot' was until quite recently the preserve of male bathers only, many of whom enjoy swimming and sun-bathing in the nude. And why not?

However, the advent of the feminist movement in recent years inevitably brought a determined invasion by some feminine activists on this bastion of male chauvinism — with some amusing and embarrassing results ! — and now the masculine 'skinny dipper' can no longer be guaranteed that male exclusivity that he hitherto enjoyed. Still, on a recent ice-cold March afternoon I happened on two or three stalwart specimens disporting themselves *au naturel*. Good luck to them — though I hesitate to think what

Thackeray's Mrs Mulholligan would have said had she been with me at the time!

For the special team of CIE civil engineers engaged in adapting and transforming the old line to meet the requirements of the new DART system, perhaps the most technically difficult section was that between Dun Laoghaire and Sandycove, where there were seven overbridges and sub-standard clearances, three of them major road bridges — Crofton Road bridge; People's Park bridge; and Sandycove Road bridge. Two alternatives were considered — (a) to lift and reconstruct the bridges and regrade the adjoining road approaches; or (b) to lower the track in the rock cutting. The second alternative was chosen, on economical and environmental grounds. This involved closing one track at a time and excavating the rock to a depth of approximately 500 mm, and replacing the track on a continuously paved concrete bed. A special paving machine was used for this work, resulting in the introduction of the first section (1.5 km) in Ireland of this new type of track.

Blackrock

'Blackrock, in Dublin, is the most celebrated sea-bathing place in the vicinity of the capital. The streets are rather confined, but the extraordinary beauty of the country residences, and of the seashore, secures to the Rock a long train of equestrian visitors, and a multiplied importation by jaunting cars. The Inns afford good accommodation. There are several roads to Bray. Pop. 1400.'
— Leigh's Road-Book of Ireland. 1832

Blackrock has changed, but not that much. The streets are still 'rather confined', which to me — a non-motorized hiker and inveterate rail traveller — is part of the charm of the place. I like the recognizable village centre amidst the sprawl of suburbia. Most everything worth viewing or visiting in the way of old places along the DART line are within a stone's throw of the stations. Blackrock is no exception. And no amount of 'multiplied importations' — how I love that phrase! — can diminish its attractions.

I never pass along its main street without seeing an elegant drunk happily churning out a scrappy melody from an old barrel organ. The drunk is crooning a patriotic air in time to the cranked-out tune; he has just borrowed the contraption from its Italian owner, gently but insistently shouldering the bemused Neapolitan to one side. The singing of the tipsy gent becomes louder. He has a fine tenor voice. The passersby smile indulgently, one or two of them pausing for a little while. A few shopkeepers come to their doors, grinning and listening and nodding with amused condescension. The Italian immigrant, matching their grins, spreads his hands and hunches his shoulders in an eloquent gesture of mild apology. *Non fa niente . . . tutti sono felici.* Everybody is happy!

Everybody, that is, except the little boy Stanislaus Joyce coming from school and who thus witnesses his father making a show of himself on the main street. The disintegration of Joyce senior has set in. He is drinking too heavily. He has flown a few too many kites — promissory notes and IOUs — each bearing the signature of John Stanislaus Joyce and all flying high and wide over the city. The moneylenders, the solicitors and the creditors have begun to haul them down, one at a time at first, then snatching at them in handfuls. It will soon be time for the Joyce family to quit their nice home at 23 Carysford Avenue, Blackrock, and to begin that long odyssey through so many parts of Dublin — more than a dozen addresses in as many years — all downward steps, as the happy-go-lucky and feckless man-about-town tries to dodge the increasing horde of shylocks and creditors. Many years later his famous son, in *A Portrait of the Artist as a Young Man,* will write of his weeping mother gazing from the window of their railway carriage and watching the two great yellow horse vans with all the family furniture lumbering heavily along the Merrion Road.

But whenever I walk down Blackrock's main street I like to picture the happy drunk and the smiling owner of the barrel organ. Was there a playful little monkey too? Had I been around at the time I think I would have joined them for a little while, practising my atrocious Italian on my grandfather's compatriot and lilting a verse or two of an Irish ballad with the man who was once described as 'the handsomest man and the boldest flirt in the city of Cork in his day'. *Tutti sono felici!*

But I doubt if I would have delayed too long in such happy company. There are so many other places in Blackrock that I wish to see. The People's Park, for instance; a delightful retreat beneath which lies part of the black limestone which once skirted the foreshore and which gives the locality its name. Nothing remains of that rock today, save for a few dark chunks that were hewn out to make part of the railway wall. I was only about seven years old when my Grandma Caprani first brought me to this park with my cousins. What stories she told us!

Even today there is a jumble of legends and history and fairytales in my mind somehow associated with the ancient stone cross, with its mysteriously carved head, standing in the Main Street. Nothing is known of its origins, though it is believed to be at least a thousand years old. And, as it is an integral part of Blackrock, my elusive memories of childhood tie it in with the story of the Cheevers family. Was it a tale that Grandma told us? I'm not sure. I can't remember.

Walter Cheevers was the Lord of Blackrock in an age when the majority of the old Anglo-Irish Catholic landlords were not lacking in responsibility towards their tenants and retainers. After the Confederate wars of the 1640s the Cromwellians dispossessed Walter and, with a 'to Hell or to Connaught' edict, banished him and his family to the unknown and infertile lands of western Ireland. In the blinding snowstorms of January 1653 Cheevers, his wife and five young children were forced out of the ancestral home. Before them lay a hundred miles of icy mud paths, white drifts, piercing cold and a vast uncertainty.

There followed seven long years of exile in a harsh region which Cromwell is reputed to have described as not possessing enough water to drown a man, enough wood to hang him, nor enough earth to bury him. Happily for Walter Cheevers and his family there were no hangings or burials. In 1660, when the Stuart monarchy was restored and Cromwell no more, Cheevers and his family were suddenly free to return to their ancestral home. How different that march back, what a triumphal procession! The church bells pealed and resounded with the joy of welcome and homecoming. Blackrock, in the evening, was ablaze with bonfires.

It may be my temperament, or something in the sea air, or it may be something of both, but even on the dullest day of winter or when the air is drenched with the melancholy of Autumn I never approach Blackrock without the expectancy of barrel organs, bonfires and bells.

But that might have something to do with its inns too, I admit. Leigh, in his oft-quoted *Road Book,* makes reference to the good qualities of Blackrock's inns 150 years ago. The present ones continue the tradition of those 18th century 'repositories' of fine spirits and haunts of merriment' known as the Three Tun Tavern, Conways, Jennetts and the Sign of the Ship. The latter had a spacious and elegant ballroom; despite its nautical title it catered for practitioners of the quadrille and the minuet, and not for those of the boisterous sailors' hornpipe, for throughout the 'season' Blackrock boasted and revelled in 'the sweets of dissipation to so high a degree that even Bath could scarce take the lead for more gaiety, amusement and bon ton'. Dublin city may have been the better town to work and scheme in, but Blackrock got all the fun; it was the seat of fashion; accessible, lively and an admirable school for scandal. It attracted all sorts.

Some there were, among the 'long train of equestrian visitors' who came riding in for the rich pickings. The sequestered and tree-lined lanes skirting the fine mansions and leading to and from the 'celebrated sea-bathing place' was ideal territory for the daring highwayman. Jannett's Tavern was the

Deepwell, Blackrock.

venue for a meeting presided over by an angry Lord Ranelagh in 1787 who invited the assembly to consider the most expeditious method of ridding the countryside around Blackrock of all highwaymen and road agents. No doubt his lordship and the assembled gentlemen had a genuine greviance, but my feelings for the romance of Blackrock are such that I cannot quite visualize the local highwaymen as anything other than a breed of gallant adventurers. I see them — dressed in surtout and tricorn hat, their black masks not entirely concealing their handsome features — sighing mysteriously over a lady's gloved hand extended from the darkness of a carriage. Before rider and horse gallop off in a white slant of moonlight there is time for a final compliment and a merry laugh — what lady would not but be happy to part with a bauble to such a charming thief? And was the immensely rich Lord Ranelagh any worse off for a lighter purse now and then? Perhaps the reality was more grim. But for me the dispossessed raparee and the highwayman will always be represented as brave, handsome, merciful, gallant to females, a hater of oppression; and if he robbed from the rich it was only to give large portions of the plunder to the poor.

A few of the fine 'country residences' still remain: Castle Dawson, now Blackrock College; Lisaniskean, the home of Lady Arabella Denny in the 1750s; Blackrock House, once the summer residence of the Lord Lieutenants; Prospect House, which became a boarding school for the sprigs of the gentry; Neptune, now Temple Hill House; many more, alas, perished

107

before the demolition squads of the modern developers of apartment complex and supermarket. Not a trace remains of the most notable, Frescati Lodge.

I walk past where Frescati used to be and I think of a brave and reckless young man and the quiet courage of his beautiful young wife. Lord Edward Fitzgerald is a figure who stands in Irish history as a symbol of dashing and romantic valour; his wife Pamela is one of its sad victims. While he was using a dozen secret addresses in efforts to elude the spies of Dublin Castle she remained at Frescati and played a kind of hide-and-seek game with her memories of brief happiness. Both were losers.

Frescati was built in the 1760s and became the home of the dowager Duchess of Leinster, Emily Fitzgerald. As the widow of Ireland's premier aristocrat Emily forsook the family's magnificent ducal seat, Carton, near Maynooth, and equally the palatial Leinster House in town. Her favourite home was Frescati. She had two additional wings put onto the original lodge to accommodate her large family. Lord Edward, the fifth son, spent most of his childhood there. He loved Frescati, later writing of 'the little book-room, with the windows open, hearing the birds sing, and the place looking beautiful'. And it was to Frescati in 1793 he took his beautiful young bride from Paris, Pamela, daughter of Madame de Genlis and the Duc D'Orleans, and thus a niece of the guillotined Louis XVI.

What a handsome and noble couple they made! Pamela must have thought that this was to be the happy-ever-after sequel to their whirlwind romance amidst the French Reign of Terror, she must have thought too that her beloved Edward welcomed this peaceful domesticity after nearly a dozen years of colourful adventures on two continents. At sixteen years of age Lord Edward had entered the army as a subaltern; he had crossed the Atlantic with his regiment, seen action in the American War of Independence, been badly wounded, then rescued and nursed back to health by Tony, his faithful black servant; there had followed a series of perilous travels in the American wilderness, a return to France, meetings with Tom Paine (author of *The Rights of Man)*, with Pamela's father and other aristocratic liberalists, with leading revolutionaries; a first-hand witnessing of the establishment of the French Republic; an enthusiastic welcome for its principles; the renunciation of his titles; being cashiered from the army as a consequence of his new-found egalitarianism; and then courtship and marriage to Pamela. And now, at 30 years of age, the handsome groom arrives in Ireland, still accompanied by his faithful manservant Tony, and with a charming and accomplished bride to help him set up home at Frescati.

A year later, after the birth of their first child, Pamela and Lord Edward are still blissfully happy and he is writing to his mother of his joy at Frescati '...I go without coat, and the birds are singing like Spring ... I have also trimmed the rose trees'. But is this the right note for a would-be revolutionary exasperated by the state of his country? Napper Tandy,

Arthur O'Connor, Seamus McNevin and other luminaries of the United Irishmen are becoming frequent visitors to Frescati. The midnight oil burns well into the early hours and casts shadows about their conspiracy. By day Lord Edward is walking 'the streets instead of riding and thence says he feels more pride in being on a level with his fellow-citizens'. Thus he goes about the town, frightening one class with his adoption of French republican ideals and fashion, his hair shorn in the manner of a revolutionary, his clothes of the same cut, and at the same time inflaming another class with his radical enthusiasm. Warm, impetuous, generous hearted, he is idolized by the common citizenry.

Pamela alone is prey to misgivings. The fear never leaves her. She has seen how events have worked out in France. Her own father had likewise made himself popular by his liberalism. He had headed the seceding noblemen who had joined the *tiers état,* had sat in the convention that had decreed the death of Louis and Marie Antoinette, had accepted the title of *Citoyen Egalite* for his part in the regicide. But the mob had turned on him just as savagely in the end and he had perished on the same guillotine as his kingly brother and at the hands of the same terrorists. Will it be the same here?

Lord Edward's cause is already lost. The spies and informers are at work and the government are offering a reward of £1,000 for his capture. He is forced to go underground, his surgeon friend Lawless organising his many hiding places. Pamela is virtually a prisoner at Frescati. From dawn to dusk she waits for word of her beloved, whipped by fearful emotions, clutching her three babes about her, the eldest child not yet four years. What is to become of them? In the midst of her misfortunes is heard a new note, the angry murmur of the common people and the sound of musket fire — an awful echo of the Bastille! — as the rebellion of 1798 quickly flames and is just as quickly and ruthlessly stamped out. And still no news of her husband. Where is he?

He has steadfastly refused to abandon the defeated men by fleeing to France as he might have done. And the rebels, for whom this aristocrat had despised and discarded his titles and sacrificed his happiness, are willingly moving him from one safe house after another — Mrs Dillon's at Portobello, the Brazen Head Inn, Gleeson the draper in Cornmarket, the Yellow Lion Tavern, Cormick's of Thomas Street, Magan's of Usher's Quay, and finally to the attic of Murphy the feather-seller at 151 Thomas Street. But Lord Edward's implacable enemy and relentless pursuer, the infamous Major Sirr, is closing in. He picks up the trail at Francis Magan's. Magan breaks down and confesses all.

On the attic stairs above the feather-seller's premises there is a faint, almost inaudible sound. A whisper, a creaking floorboard, or a tip-toe in the dark? Even as Lord Edward Fitzgerald reaches for the only weapon at hand, a dagger, the door is suddenly flung inward and Sirr and his men rush into the room. The rebel leader has the heart of a lion. He lunges at them, ready to fight any man of equal courage. There is a fierce, brief struggle in which he deftly accounts for two of Sirr's cohorts before a pistol shot from the Major, at almost point blank range, blasts him back against the wall. Grieviously wounded, the dagger falls from his hand and his arms are pinioned by his captors.

From Murphy's house — a plaque marks the site today — Lord Edward is conveyed to Newgate Prison. He is flung into a dirty cell and there, with barbarous neglect, he languishes for two weeks before dying of his wounds. Not until the very last moments are his relatives permitted to visit him. Pamela, who has been so persistent in her demands, has not only been excluded from the gaol, but has been already deported from Ireland before the death of her beloved Edward. She will never return....

A dark curtain of silence descends on Frescati Lodge. Perhaps, in a way, it is better that the house has vanished. Time dealt neither lightly nor kindly with it or its occupants....

When I head back for Booterstown or Blackrock stations the intense sentimental interests associated with the locality are slowly overtaken by soft echoes — a grandmother's voice recounting old tales and legends to children in a sunlit park ... the pealing of church bells, and the throb of bonfires, muffled by the distance of three centuries ... a ghostly hurdy-gurdy tune being coaxed out of an Italian street organ by a happy drunk ... and, most poignantly, the 'birds singing like Spring' above the laurels and the rose trees of Frescati....

Booterstown

Booterstown, both as a rail station and as a semi-rural suburban locality, seems to have been at the centre of every legal wrangle in the days of the early railway. Might this have had something to do with Booterstown's unique position of being the mid-point on the line between Kingstown/Dunleary and Westland Row? Being fired upon from both sides, as it were?

Trouble came from every quarter — petitions from influential church-goers who objected to the railway's 'unremitting traffic' on the Sabbath; the Post Office wishing the railway to carry the local Penny Post and the mails to and from the 'intervening village of Booterstown', but declining to pay £600 per annum as requested by the railway company for the said carriage and suggesting instead that the mail guard sit on the 'roof of the carriage with a box at his feet for the mails'. Then there was the case of the railway director driving past the 'Coach and Horses' pub on the Merrion Road and being aghast to see one of the company's locomotives standing idle and unattended on the tracks. Where was the crew? He found them in the tavern, knocking back cider and porter. Needless to remark the thirsty railmen were reported and hauled before the board; there was a hearing, grave warnings issued, heavy fines imposed and new rules of behaviour drawn up.

And what of Mr Kenyon's dog? In August 1854, when the board had just introduced a fare of threepence for each dog carried, it was discovered that a certain Mr Kenyon of Booterstown had devised his own little stratagem for dealing with the new regulation. Kenyon had a thrifty mind and a well-trained pet. At Booterstown station he'd purchase his ticket, wait on the platform, and leave Fido lying low in the bushes. Once Kenyon had boarded the train and taken his seat he'd give a short, low whistle. Just as the train began to move off Fido would streak from the bushes and leap in through the open-sided, doorless 3rd class carriage. Reverse procedure at Westland Row. Kenyon would stroll nonchalantly through the ticket barrier, the dog following at a distance on the platform. Then another low whistle, and Fido would rejoin his master outside on the street.

The railway staff at both stations soon became aware of this little bit of sharp practice. The matter was reported to the higher-ups. This in turn led to a complete re-examination of the company's bye-laws in an effort to bring Kenyon and his cur to heel. Judge the dismay of the directors when their legal advisers informed them that they had, in fact, no legal right to charge for dogs.

A much more far-reaching legal wrangle — and one which quickly escalated from an incident at the station one morning, via the Dublin courts, to the House of Commons, and then to hurried legislation in the form of 'The Cheap Trains Act 1858! — was set in motion by another resident of Booterstown, a local market gardener named Rice. When the station clerk charged Rice two and a half pence for a 3rd class fare to Westland Row, as was customary, the former must have been somewhat taken aback when Rice pointed out in no uncertain terms that the 'Regulation of Railways Act 1844 clearly stated that the fare or charge for each 3rd class passenger shall not exceed one penny for each mile travelled', and that the said Act made no mention of divisions or fractions of a penny, and that, moreover, while the distance to Westland Row was more than two and a half miles it certainly

Lapwing, Booterstown Marsh.

wasn't three, and thus the correct charge should be no more than twopence!

The clerk insisted on the full fare. Rice paid, then took the matter to his solicitors, and instructed them to institute legal proceedings against the new Dublin & Wicklow Railway for the sum of one halfpenny, wrongfully overcharged. The Court of Common Pleas found in favour of Rice, despite lengthy and detailed arguments presented by the railway attornies. The matter was hastily passed on to the Board of Trade in London and thence to Westminster for correcting legislation and the 'Cheap Trains Act 1858', which laid down that one penny was to be the fare for a mile or so, and a halfpenny for any odd portion between a half mile and a mile.

Rice, it should be added, was one of the more energetic members of the Waysiders' Association, a league of railway users, set up to fight for what they regarded as their rights, and which frequently quarrelled with the Dublin & Wicklow Railway for the manner in which it conducted the management of the Dublin to Kingstown line.

At Booterstown archaeologists have found traces of the ancient double ditch which once delineated the curious defensive territory of the 'Pale'. The Pale was largely confined to the flat coastal plains stretching from the Dublin mountains in the south to the edges of Carlingford Lough in the north, and inside its protective bulwarks the early Norman settlers lived while keeping a wary eye on their Gaelic neighbours outside. Immediately beyond the Pale were the hotly disputed 'march lands', over which invader and native held sway at various times in the turbulent 12th and 13th centuries. The double ditch ran roughly parallel with the coastline from Dalkey to Donnybrook, then swung inland in a broad swathe to take in parts of Kildare, Meath and Louth, where it met the sea again at Dundalk. The 'march lands' should not be confused with 'marshlands'. The 'marches' were boundaries, a kind of buffer zone between the Norman-held territory and that of the natives.

Booterstown Marsh, on the other hand (lying directly between the DART line and the main Dun Laoghaire/Dublin Road) is a nature reserve, one of the many roosting areas for thousands of birds using the mudflats of Dublin Bay as a source of food. Greater Dublin, in fact, is probably unique among the metropolitan areas of western Europe in that it includes within its boundaries two extensive wild life sanctuaries, the Bull Island and Booterstown Marsh. The latter, with its brackish mixture of fresh and salt water and its plashy muds, is an important wetland for many species of wildfowl and waders. It attracts all the main species — the noisy, conspicuous black-and-white oyster-catcher; the streaky-brown curlew with his long curved bill and his eerie cry; the lapwing, the teal, the snipe and the shoveler. From the DART window they can be seen foraging relentlessly on the rich plant and animal life of Booterstown's marshy tract.

And directly beyond the marsh, on the Rock Road, may be seen the home of Ireland's most celebrated tenor, John Count McCormack. The house,

Glena, Booterstown (John Count McCormack's house).

Glena, is distinguishable by its little cone-topped, fenestrated mini-tower to one side of the steps leading up to the halldoor.

Born in Athlone in 1884, McCormack's popularity as a concert artist was unrivalled in the 1920s and 30s. It enabled him to amass a fortune estimated at over a million dollars in pre-1939 money terms. His singing career began with a *Feis Cheol* gold medal win when he was only eighteen, after which he was encouraged by his teacher to continue his studies in Milan. There his lyrical voice, perfect diction and consummate musicianship won him early success on the operatic stage. But as Italian opera-lovers favoured home-grown tenors to foreigners, and found the consonant-laden name 'McCormack' difficult to pronounce, he made his stage debut under the name 'Giovanni Foli' (the stage name a tribute to his fiancee, Lily Foley). There followed even greater success — and now under his rightful name — in Naples, London, New York, Boston and Chicago. By 1912 McCormack had toured the world with 21 roles in his operatic repertoire.

Like his illustrious contemporary, Enrico Caruso, McCormack was fortunate in that his singing career coincided with the introduction of sound recording and the gramophone craze (and later, radio broadcasting), thus bringing his exquisite singing to millions; but, unlike Caruso, the Irishman abandoned opera after 1913 in favour of the concert stage. His repertoire of classical and Irish songs, sentimental ballads and Moore's Melodies, assured

113

his popularity in every city where Irish emigrants resided — from San Francisco to London, New York to Sydney. McCormack was generous with his time and talents in fund-raising for charities, particularly during both world wars, when he gave many concerts on behalf of the Red Cross.

Although he became a US citizen in 1917 McCormack always maintained close links with his homeland and spent his latter years in Ireland, first at Moore Abbey, Monasterevin, where he kept a string of expensive racehorses, and in the last two years at Glena, Booterstown. He died in September 1945 with one of his greatest ambitions unfulfilled — despite all his immense fame, popularity, wealth and racing stables, he never succeeded in winning the Derby.

The rail traveller may just be able to discern, between the two front windows of Glena house, the commemorative plaque set up there by McCormack's many Irish admirers and music lovers.

Sydney Parade

Whenever I step onto the platform at Sydney Parade station — a rather ordinary, though not unattractive suburban halt — I find it difficult to imagine that this site was once intended to be one of the major hubs of a vast plan to ring Dublin and its environs with an intricate network of inter-connected railways. Oh yes, great things were planned for Sydney Parade in the golden age of Victorian rail expansion. A scheme was sanctioned by Parliament in the 1860s which would have connected this quiet maritime area on the main Dublin-Kingstown line with an important suburban branch to the inland suburb of Ranelagh. It was further envisaged that the same main line would diverge at Sydney Parade, run to Ringsend, and from there (via a tunnel under the Liffey) traverse the northern suburbs and link all the then mainline railways: the GNR, the MGW, the GS & W, the Dublin South Suburban, and the DW & WR. But, like so many great Irish plans and ideas, nothing ever came of this grandiose scheme for a 'Dublin Trunk Connecting Railway', and thus Sydney Parade was relegated to being nothing more important than a modest suburban halt.

Ordinary, modest, suburban? Yes and no. For, on reflection, Sydney Parade will always be tinged with a little romantic sadness, associated as it is with characters involved in two tragic deaths — one of those associations tenuous, though factual; the other immediate, though fictional. The tenuous link with the death of Michael Collins at Beal-na-Blath, August 22 1921, is provided by the fact that his companion-in-arms on that fateful day was General Emmet Dalton, who, at one time, lived at 25 Sydney Parade Avenue. The immediate, though fictional, death was that of the tragic and passionate Emily Sinico in Joyce's *A Painful Case*.

In a personal narrative of the final hours of Collins's death Emmet Dalton wrote in the *Freeman's Journal:*

'It was now about a quarter past seven, and the light was failing. We were speeding along the open road on our way to Macroom. Our motor cyclist scout was about 50 yards in front of the Crossley tender, which we followed at the same interval in the touring car. Close behind us came the armoured car. We had just reached a part of the road which was commanded by hills on all sides ... when a sudden and heavy fusillade of machine-gun and rifle fire swept the road in front and behind us, shattering the windscreen of our car.

I shouted to the driver — "Drive like hell!" But the Commander-in-Chief, placing his hand on the man's shoulder, said — "Stop! Jump out and we'll fight them."

We leaped from the car, and took what cover we could behind the little mud bank on the left-hand side of the road. It seemed that the greatest volume of fire was coming from the concealed roadway on our left-hand side. The armour car now backed up the road and opened a heavy machine-gun fire at the hidden ambushers. General Collins and I were lying within arm's length of each other. Captain Dolan, who had been on the back of the armoured car, together with our two drivers, was several yards further down the road to my right. We opened a rapid rifle fire on our seldom visible enemies. About fifty or sixty yards further down the road, and round a bend, we could hear that our machine gunners and riflemen were also heavily engaged.

We continued this fire fight for about 20 minutes without suffering any casualties, when a lull in the enemy's attack became noticeable. General Collins now jumped up to his feet and walked over behind the armoured car, obviously to obtain a better view of the enemy's position. He remained there, firing occasional shots and using the car as cover. Suddenly I heard him shout "Come on boys! There they are, running up the road." I immediately opened fire upon two figures that came in view on the opposite road.

When I next turned round the Commander-in-Chief had left the car position, and had run about fifteen yards back up the road. Here he dropped into the prone firing position, and opened up on our retreating enemies.'

General Dalton goes on to describe how he, Captain Dolan and Commandant Sean O'Connell took up firing positions on the road further down. Presently the firing of Michael Collins ceased, and Dalton heard, or fancied he heard, a faint cry of 'Emmet!'. He then describes how he and O'Connell....

'rushed to the spot with a dreadful fear clutching our hearts. We found our beloved Chief and friend lying motionless in a firing position, firmly gripping his rifle, across which his head was resting. There was a fearful gaping wound at the base of the skull behind the right ear. We immediately saw that General Collins was almost beyond human aid. He could not speak to us.

O'Connell now knelt down beside the dying but still conscious Chief, whose eyes were wide open and normal, and he whispered into the ear of the fast-sinking man the words of the Act of Contrition. For this he was rewarded by a slight pressure of the hand.

Meanwhile I knelt beside them both, and kept up bursts of rapid fire, which I continued whilst O'Connell dragged the Chief across the road and behind the armoured car. Then, with my heart torn with sorrow and despair, I ran to the Chief's side. Very gently I raised his head on my knee and tried to bandage his wound, but, owing to the awful size of it, this proved very difficult.

I had not completed my grevious task when the big eyes quickly closed, and the cold pallor of death overspread the General's face. How can I describe the feelings that were mine at that bleak hour, kneeling in the mud of a country road not twelve miles from Clonakilty, with the still bleeding head of the Idol of Ireland resting on my arm.'

And when the evening light is failing at Sydney Parade station, the DART traveller, if he has imagination enough, can give it a little rein and join Mr James Duffy of Chapelizod (cashier of a private bank in Baggot Street) as he plucks the fringe of the buff *Mail* from his pocket and reads 'the paragraph again by the failing light of the window. He read it not aloud, but moving his lips as a priest does when he reads the prayers *Secreto*. This was the paragraph:

DEATH OF A LADY AT SYDNEY PARADE
A PAINFUL CASE

Today at the City of Dublin Hospital the Deputy Coroner in the absence of Mr Leverett, held an inquest on the body of Mrs Emily Sinico, aged forty-three years, who was killed at Sydney Parade Station yesterday evening. The evidence showed that the deceased lady while attempting to cross the line, was knocked down by the engine of the ten o'clock slow train from Kingstown, thereby sustaining injuries of the head and right side which led to her death.

Mr Duffy reads on: '... The deceased had been in the habit of crossing the lines late at night from platform to platform and, in view of certain other circumstances of the case, he did not think the railway officials were to blame ... Captain Sinico, of Leoville, Sydney Parade, husband of the deceased, also gave evidence. He was not in Dublin at the time of the accident as he had arrived only that morning from Rotterdam. They had been married for twenty-two years and had lived happily until about two years ago, when his wife began to be rather intemperate in her habits ...

Miss Mary Sinico said that of late her mother had been in the habit of going out at night to buy spirits...'.

Four years earlier Duffy had met Emily Sinico at a concert in the Rotunda. He had been struck by her appearance — 'oval face ... bosom of a certain fullness ... the eyes were very dark blue and steady. Their gaze began with a defiant note, but was confused by what seemed a deliberate swoon of the pupil into the iris, revealing for an instant a temperament of great sensibility'. It was to be the first of many meetings. He went often to her little cottage outside Dublin; often they spent their evenings alone, for her husband was captain of a mercantile boat plying between Dublin and Holland. Little by little he attached the fervent nature of Emily more closely to him, entangling her thoughts with his, lending her books, providing her with ideas, sharing his intellectual life and theories with her. Emily listened to all he had to say. 'The end of these discourses was that one night, during which she had shown every sign of unusual excitement, Mrs Sinico caught up his hand passionately and pressed it to her cheek'.

Poor Emily — that impulsive gesture was her undoing. It's spontaneity threatened the equanimity of Mr James Duffy's orderly little life, it menaced his preciseness. He didn't visit her again, choosing to write instead and asking her to meet him in a little cake shop at the Parkgate. 'It was cold autumn weather, but in spite of the cold they wandered up and down the roads of the Park for nearly three hours. They agreed to break off their intercourse: every bond, he said, is a bond of sorrow. When they came out of the Park they walked in silence towards the tram; but here she began to tremble so violently that, fearing another collapse on her part, he bade her good-bye quickly and left her.'

He never saw her again, keeping away from the concerts where they used to meet. And now, suddenly after four years, this awful paragraph in the *Mail*. 'The whole narrative of her death revolted him and it revolted him to think that he had ever spoken to her of what he held sacred ... not merely had she degraded herself; she had degraded him. He saw the squalid tract of her vice, miserable and malodorous. His soul's companion! He thought of the hobbling wretches whom he had seen carrying cans and bottles to be filled by the barman. Just God, what an end!'.

And what an end for Mr James Duffy, cashier of a private bank. That night he enters the Park and walks under the gaunt trees where he had walked with Emily four years before. The furtive lovers lying on the slope of the Magazine Hill fill him with despair. 'He gnawed the rectitude of his life; he felt that he had been outcast from life's feast. One human being had seemed to love him and he had denied her life and happiness; he had sentenced her to ignominy, a death of shame. He knew that the prostrate creatures down by the wall were watching him and wished him gone. No one wanted him ... he listened again: perfectly silent. He felt that he was alone.'

Sydney Parade — ordinary, modest, suburban? Yes, maybe. But to catch the sad echo of old tragedies — one real, and the other no less so for having been created by James Joyce — one should always visit the station and walk the length of the platform in the failing light of an autumn evening....

Loop Line

Back once more to Pearse (Westland Row) via Sandymount and Lansdowne Road. Immediately before the Dodder bridge leading into the latter station an astute DART traveller can just about make out the break in the stone wall skirting the line where the old RDS rail siding left the mainline and curved into the Ballsbridge platform.

And directly after leaving Pearse station we pass *through* Trinity College. To the best of my knowledge the DART line must be the only railroad in the world to actually run through part of a university. Admittedly, only a small part — nipping in and out, as it were, over about 500 feet of the university's property at the corner of Westland Row and Pearse Street, and yet affording us a fine view of some of the college buildings. The DART, or Loop Line, viaduct curves gently across the Botany Bay area of the university, giving us a view of the Parade Ground and the Botany, Physics, Physiology and Biochemistry buildings etc.

Trinity College is one of the few universities in the world which teaches as many branches of learning as the word *universitas* implies. Modern universities developed from the European universities of the Middle Ages, institutions that grew out of the natural tendency of learned men to gather together for mutual help and study. This led to a process of segregation in suitable districts, often at certain schools connected with cathedrals or abbeys. Such a university for Dublin was originally projected in 1311, but did not flourish till the reign of Elizabeth I, from whom Archbishop Usher obtained its charter. Dr Adam Loftus, Archbishop of Dublin, was the first Provost, and Usher, Chaloner and Moyne were the first Fellows.

I find myself once again crossing the Loop Line and looking down on the bridge named after every Irish nationalist's favourite Orangeman, Isaac Butt. What a character, was Butt — a genial, generous, improvident tippler and gambler, not one whit like the dour, thrifty, hard-working humourless stereotype of the Ulster Protestant. He was constantly and consistently ignoring the bailiffs, the tradesmens' bills and the threatening letters that dogged his colourful life. He delighted in gregarious company, in giving rollicking parties at his home in Eccles Street, and in performing parlour conjuring tricks for his many and varied guests.

A Donegalman, Butt founded the *Dublin University Magazine* and thereby discovered and gave an outlet for the literary talents of Le Fanu and Lever, pursued his own talented career as a much sought-after barrister, took silk, was elected to Westminster as a Unionist, defended the Young Irelanders and the Fenians, and, in the process, founded the Irish Home Rule Party almost by accident. He remained its leader until ousted by Parnell and when he died in 1879 Dubliners clamoured to have the latest bridge over their river, then in the course of construction, named after him.

The bridge, which was rebuilt and widened in 1932, was, until a few years ago — and prior to the erection of the Matt Talbot Bridge and the East Link toll bridge — known to an older generation of Dubliners as 'the new bridge'. And it was one of that generation — a friend of mine, and a lifelong communist — who once remarked to me with a kind of wry disillusionment: 'this country will never be truly socialist, and do you know why? Because it's the only country that ever tried to have a strike-breakin' scab canonised by the Church.'

He was referring — somewhat erroneously and unjustly — to Matt Talbot, who was born in 1856 in the heart of what was then Dublin's northside slums. Talbot, a reformed alcoholic who afterwards adopted a life of penetential asceticism and mortification, was once employed as a storeman in T & C Martin's timberyard on the North Wall. During the great labour strike and lock-out of 1913 Talbot was accused (by, among others, Sean O'Casey) of being a blackleg and strike breaker. Talbot always maintained that he supported the workers' cause but that he was opposed to violent picketing and intimidation.

Be that as it may, there was little love lost between O'Casey, the pacifist who was once the secretary of the Irish Citizen Army, and Talbot the inveterate drunkard who suddenly renounced his former way of life and replaced it with a life of prayer and piety. When O'Casey's plays *The Shadow of a Gunman* (1923) and *Juno and the Paycock* (1925) took the theatre world by storm with their depiction of the squalor of the Dublin tenements and the horrors of rebellion and civil war, Talbot expressed his disapproval of what he considered to be a denigration of 'decent Dubliners' in the playwright's characters. He was dead by the time O'Casey's *The Plough and the Stars* had its premier at the Abbey in 1926. Perhaps it was just as well, for the play contained a real-life character — or caricature, Talbot might have said — of one of Talbot's erstwhile boozing pals, one Jack 'Fluther' Good. Fluther too considered it a caricature and a libel. He took an action against the playwright for what he called 'definition of character', and was awarded damages of £50 — a not inconsiderable sum for a drinking man at a time when the pint cost only a few pence.

In 1925, the year before O'Casey finally turned his back on Dublin's coterie of literary begrudgers and set out for London, Matt Talbot dropped dead in Granby Lane on his way to mass in Dominick Street. When his body was examined in Jervis Street Hospital rusted chains and knotted ropes were found deeply embedded in his emaciated flesh. Neither friend nor relative had been aware of this self-inflicted penance and now Catholic Dublin was suddenly agog with stories of the saintly mysticism of this unknown and unskilled labourer. His one-roomed home at 17 Upper Rutland Street — since demolished, although a bronze slab commemorates the spot beside a new block of flats named Matt Talbot Court — quickly became a place of pilgrimage and veneration. In 1952 the Holy See commenced the apostolic process of canonisation after his body was exhumed and pronounced 'the Servant of God'. His coffin can be seen in a special vault in the Church of Our Lady of Lourdes, Sean McDermott Street, his name on the new bridge down river from the Custom House.

And O'Casey's trilogy of plays can still be seen on the Abbey stage from time to time. And Fluther Good? He has a pub named after him in Ballybough. And perhaps he has the last word, as written for him by O'Casey: 'Fluther (gulping down the drink that remains in his glass, and rushing out). Come on, man, this is too grand to be missed!'

And reference to the 1913 Lock-Out and the Irish Citizen Army must inevitably draw our gaze to the most prominent building beside the Loop Line — Liberty Hall, Dublin's first 'skyscraper' and the headquarter's of Ireland's largest trade union, the ITGWU. Built in 1960 on the site of the original Liberty Hall (which, in turn, had been the old Northumberland Hotel) its story is too well known to be recounted here — the citadel from which Big Jim Larkin, that passionate, demagogic champion of the oppressed, flung down the gauntlet to Dublin's employers and capitalists, and from the steps of which he inspired the workers to fight all forms of despotism and exploitation; in its meeting rooms his sister Delia Larkin and Countess Markievicz set up soup kitchens to feed the hungry children and the womenfolk of the strikers; in its cellars, on an old Wharfedale flatbed press, the Proclamation of the Irish Republic was printed on the eve of the Rising; and from its hallway James Connolly and the men of the Irish Citizen Army — the world's first organised army of the proletariat — marched out to battle on Easter Monday morning, 1916. And looking at Liberty Hall (Dublin's highest building) today one cannot help recalling that the ITGWU began life in 1909 in a tenement room just across the river in Townsend Street with nothing more in the way of property or furnishings than 'a table, a couple of chairs, two empty bottles and a candle'.

Before the DART returns once more to Connolly Station there is time to view the new Irish Life Assurance building complex at the junction of Lower Abbey Street, Lower Gardiner Street and Beresford Place. In its forecourt stands an ornamental fountain surmounted by sculptor Oisin Kelly's magnificent 'Chariot of Life' piece, a powerful representation of galloping horses, chariot and charioteer standing foursquare and pulling manfully on imaginary reins. No sooner was it unveiled in July 1982 when the lineal mental descendants of those wags who dubbed the Custom House statues across the way 'the Three Stooges' had christened the Irish Life sculpture the 'Look Ma, no reins!' statue.

Enough said.

Connolly (Amiens St) to Killester

When William Dargan, engineer and entrepreneur, set out on his vastly ambitious scheme of laying out almost every railway line in Ireland — connecting Dublin first with Dun Laoghaire, then with Drogheda, later with Belfast, Galway and Cork — the newspapers of the day carried regular reports of protests and objections by resident groups, traders and influential landowners. Every mile of track was matched with a myriad of problems. Even after the various termini — the present day Pearse (Westland Row), Connolly (Amiens Street), Heuston (Kingsbridge) etcetera — were completed, Dargan, the railway magnates and the city fathers were faced with the almost insoluble problem of linking up such stations.

One proposal was for an 'elevated railway' running from Westland Row to Kingsbridge, a route following the line of the Liffey. The rail barons and the aldermen were enthusiastic. The public much less so. To give the citizens an idea of the advantages and the appearance of the proposed scheme a massive temporary wooden bridge was built across Westmoreland Street. The organisers asked the public for a frank and considered opinion. They got it. The structure was hastily removed. The Westland Row-Kingsbridge link was scrapped, much to the delight of the cabmen and jarveys whose livelihood would have suffered. It was fifty years — 1891 — before the rail companies and the Corporation risked building the Loop Line bridge over the Liffey and connecting Westland Row with Amiens Street.

The latter Terminus, at its inception in the 1840s, caused a similar furore.. The original plan for the Great Northern Railway envisaged a major station on the site of what is now Clery's, O'Connell Street, with a line running from there to Custom House Docks, then across the North Lotts, then by embankment across the sea to the Sheds in Clontarf, then a swing back inland across the green pastures and skirting St Anne's Estate, to come out at Raheny near the present Church of All Saints. The first group of strenuous objectors were the Dublin traders and merchants; then the residents of fashionable Clontarf; the final 'nay-sayer' was Sir Benjamin Lee Guinness of the brewing family. As proprietor of St Anne's and as the public benefactor who had restored St Patrick's Cathedral at a cost of £150,000 Sir Benjamin had a lot of 'clout'. The plan was abandoned. The terminus was eventually sited on the open ground of what had once been a pound for stray animals to the east of the present Amiens Street. The line was thus moved more inland and ran roughly parallel to the new North Strand Road through an area scattered with cottages, artisan dwellings and new suburban villas. Shutting out altogether the view of the sea, it made a misnomer of places like Bayview Avenue and Fairview, which Dalton (just before the building of the railway), described as follows: 'The Pidgeon House and Light House stand out as if insulated in the bay, while the Wicklow and Dublin mountains appear to connect with Howth, and completely environ a space that, but for the intrusion of the sails and steam funnels, might be deemed a noble lake.'

Though replete with numerous historical associations there is little of interest for the viewer/rail passenger until the Tolka River is reached. The entire area from Connolly station to the Tolka was called the North Lotts, or 'Newfoundland', on account of having been reclaimed from the sea. Bounded by the North Wall of the Liffey, East Wall, North Strand and the Tolka, it earned its name from the fact that in 1717 the Corporation members drew lots for the distribution among themselves of the reclaimed land. The coming of the railway more than a century later not only enriched some of their descendants but changed the condition and topography of the reclamation; between the sea and the canal area 'Newfoundland' was transformed by the junction of several railways into a chaos of thoroughfares and little streets.

There was a certain unintentional chaos too in the names of some of these thoroughfares. As a child — and faithfully memorizing the injunctions of the Penny Catechism! — we could never quite fathom the reason for three adjacent roads being christened Faith, Hope and Stoney. What had become

The Casino, Marino.

122

of Charity? Was it a warning of some sort — did too much charity result in being 'stoney-broke' and penniless? Years later we learned that Stoney Road, west of the rail line, was called after Dr Bindon Stoney, chief engineer to the port, who carried out the extension and Basin at the North Wall on so grand a scale. He designed a diving bell inside which workmen were sent down to the sea bed to build the North Wall extension. Under Dr Stoney's direction a dredging plant was also constructed, larger than had been in use anywhere up to that time. Barges for conveying material out to sea carried 1,000 tons, whereas those on the Clyde and Tyne, considered the most up-to-date, only carried half that amount.

Stoney Road runs parallel and immediately to the west of the railway embankment and joins East Wall Road at the Tolka bridge. Just as the Dodder in spate demolished the railway bridge at Lansdowne Road in 1834, so too the bridge carrying the old GNR railway line was washed away by flood waters on December 9th, 1954. A severe rainstorm over two days, plus

high tides, caused the Tolka river to overflow its banks. The flood waters rushed through Ballybough and the North Strand Road, causing widespread havoc and leaving over a 1,000 people temporarily homeless. Fortunately, there were no fatalities. Rail traffic was conducted from the old Clontarf station pending the erection of a temporary bridge at the time.

From the Tolka we again pass the rear of Fairview Park and the DART maintenance depot, and once more reach the skew bridge crossing over the Clontarf Road.

And from the skew bridge we catch a first sight of storied Marino Crescent on the left — just in off the junction of Howth Road and Clontarf Road — with the north-eastern wing of the Crescent now refurbished as luxury flats with striking mansard roofs, and the centre and western wing still retaining the original Georgian facade. It is impossible to glimpse Marino Crescent without experiencing that delicious sensation of childhood of opening a book of fairytales — no, a book of ghost stories! — for a number of important writers of the *genre* have intimate connections with it, Bram Stoker, William Carleton and Oscar Wilde. The houses of the Crescent echo with ghosts; they are a tale in themselves. They are, moreover, a monument to spite and architectural tit-for-tat.

When an enterprising builder/painter named Ffoliott decided on building the elegant seaside crescent in the 1790s he immediately ran foul of one of the most powerful men in Ireland, James Caulfield, Earl of Charlemont. An aristocrat and an aesthete, Charlemont had spent an ample fortune making his Marino estate the last word in grandeur and elegance. Macauley said of him that 'he gave the tone to the society of the age'. His house of Portland stone was extensively embellished by the eminent architects of the time and had a 60 foot long art gallery housing many of the art treasures collected by Charlemont on his Grand Tour. The centrepiece of the magnificent gardens at Marino was an ornate temple which the Earl had commissioned by the leading Roman architects and which had been constructed regardless of expense. As to the gardens themselves — Mrs Delaney, Swift's friend, was astonished at the variety of their trees and shrubs and the artificially-constructed lake, on the banks of which rare and gorgeous peacocks strutted. Add to all this the perfect representation of classical architecture known as the Casino — all that now remains of the Earl's elegant lifestyle — every stone of which is so meticulously carved that the masons estimated each at the value of a townland. But to those who came to dine at Charlemont's table and to rejoice in witty and cultivated talk — men like Grattan, Curran, Barrington — the *pièce-de-résistance* at Marino was surely the unrivalled view of Dublin Bay. All agreed with the Earl that he had a veritable gem in this wonderful panorama....

Until, of course, this vulgar little builder Ffoliott came along with his abominable and philistinic scheme to build the Crescent right smack in the foreground of the Earl's unrivalled view of the bay! This would never do!

We get some idea of the political power and privileged position of the Ascendancy class in the 18th century when we learn that the City Council once met a complaint of Charlemont's that the main road to Clontarf was too close to his lands, and therefore would they kindly have it shifted elsewhere. The city fathers immediately complied. Little wonder then that Lord Charlemont — either through the advice of his lawyer friends, or the discovery of some forgotten property right, or more probably the assistance of a compliant City Council — was happy to learn that he could quite easily baulk the tiresome little builder by exacting a toll on all goods conveyed over the narrow Clontarf road hemmed in on one side by the sea and on the other by the high walls of Marino estate. Thus, with the power to levy an exorbitant toll on every single brick, nail, slate and plank, Charlemont appeared to have effectively thwarted Ffoliott.

No, not quite — the builder's ire was roused. He had one or two tricks up his sleeve also. He quickly arranged to have all his material re-directed to Ringsend, there loaded on barges and then transported across the water to the foreshore just below Marino House. His master stroke of spiteful vengeance was to have the design of the crescent-shaped terrace of houses altered, leaving the elegant facade untouched, but planning the rear — and therefore the view permanently presented to Lord Charlmont's outraged eye and aesthetic sensibilities! — built in a terrible hodge-podge of asymmetrical chimneys, crooked roof lines, unaligned windows, jutting and irregular return-rooms and outhouses. *Touche!*

His lordship, already in declining health and conscious that the expenses of building Marino House and the nearby Casino would cripple his estate for all time, could not bear this final indignity. He left Marino for the warmer clime of the continent and died there in 1799.

A sharp eye can still discern the unprepossessing rear of the Crescent — a glimpse, as it were, of Ffoliott's revenge — just before the DART reaches the next bridge, a low metal affair spanning the Howth Road. And only a very perceptive and knowledgeable eye can discern the faint outlines of where Clontarf Railway Station once stood immediately after the same metal bridge. Built at the turn of the century and closed down in the mid-1950s, scarcely a vestige of the station remains today. A great pity, that. Apart from the boon to modern commuters what a wonderful jumping off place it would provide for modern 'ghost-hunters'.

And the place to start such a ghost hunt is surely Harry Byrne's turn-of-the-century pub just a few hundred yards up the road from the metal bridge and the vanished station. When darkness descends on this stretch of road, where pale lamps hang above the wooded gardens and cast shadows on the entrances to secluded villas, it is peopled with ghosts and the makers of ghost stories. In Harry Byrne's — the pub is only about a fifteen minute walk back from the next station, Killester — I first learned of the ghosts of Marino Crescent and their creators more than 35 years ago. The pub itself — red-

The Crescent, Marino.

bricked, wood-panelled and echoing with old tales — could well be the setting for an Edwardian melodrama; through the frosted glass windows one can almost glimpse the silhouetted figure of a hooked-nosed man with a drooping pipe, deerstalker hat and caped topcoat. It's the sort of place where one expects the door to swing open with a swirl of fog and to see the Baker Street sleuth and his faithful Dr Watson march in and make for the gleaming bar.

The late Harry Byrne — as genial a publican as ever pulled an excellent pint, God rest him! — once introduced me (a youthful scribbler) to an octogenarian 'literary gentleman' at the counter. The latter told me how the pub was built on the site of an earlier *shebeen*, Biddy Carolan's, which was

undoubtedly one of those taverns in the Killester/Clontarf area mentioned in an 1835 *Commission of Inquiry into the State of the Poor* as 'highly injurious to the morality of the lower orders'. It was almost certainly the nearest tavern to Marino Crescent, my octogenarian friend averred, and therefore the one visited by the illustrious writers who dwelt there, namely the historian Martin Haverty who lived at 21, William Carleton at 3, and Bram Stoker at 15. Did I know of them? No, not really. Well, the elderly literary gentleman recounted their tales, and urged me to visit the Crescent — preferably on a dark wintry night! I can do no better than pass on his advice.

Visit the Crescent — a brisk and energetic half-hour walk from Connolly

Station, a more casual half-hour from Killester, or by taking a bus from either — and do so on a November evening when it is murky with fog and sinister shadows, and when the harmless figures emerging from the fog on the pavement fronting the Crescent park might very well be the ghosts of whom Harry Byrne's octogenarian spoke. The ghosts crowd about you, looming out of the dark and then vanishing. It isn't too difficult to visualize Carleton at the window of No 3 leaning into the glowing orb of an oil-lamp and feverishly writing those awful scenes in the *Ribbonman:* '...the approach throws forward the shadows of some fearful evil ... I entered and advanced, the echo of my footsteps rang through the building with a lonely distinctness, which added to the solemnity and the mystery of the circumstances about me....'

Carleton did most of his early writing at the Crescent in an effort to support his impoverished wife and daughters. As a young man he had walked from his native Tyrone to the capital, a penniless itinerant who had seen at first hand the rotting bodies of Ribbonmen hanging from gibbets at many a crossroad. He knew Ireland and the Irish intimately, and his eye-witness accounts of famine, murder, evictions, dirt and drunkenness — some of which may have been gleaned at Biddy Carolan's just up the road! — while it offended Catholic and nationalist susceptibilities made him a prolific and successful novelist, who, at 60 years of age in 1855, was finally able to quit the Crescent lodgings and move into a more opulent residence in Rathgar.

Stoker and Wilde had similar childhood echoes of horror. The former, at an early age, had absorbed his mother's blood-chilling tales of the cholera epidemic of 1832 when coffin-makers, touting for business, came knocking at the cottage doors of her native Sligo. So great was the people's fear of the plague, according to Stoker's mother, that some unfortunates were actually coffined and buried alive. Such legends of the 'living dead' were allied to Stoker's boyhood reading of the lurid gothic novels of Charles Maturin and Sheridan Le Fanu — especially the latter's vampire tale *Camilla* — and combined to shape the future literary output of the author of *Dracula*.

Wilde, as a boy, had woken in the dead of night to the wails of what he thought was a dog in distress, only to be informed that it was a banshee heralding impending death. He was 12 when his sister Isola died suddenly. He kept a lock of her hair and later wrote: 'It was my first introduction to the horrors of pain, the lurking tragedies of life'. When the lurking tragedies finally laid him low in a Parisian lodging thirty-three years later the envelope containing the lock of his little sister's hair was found among his few possessions.

Sad, these literary ghosts of the Crescent....

Nor is it too difficult to catch a fleeting view of the twenty year old Wilde standing disconsolately at the railings of the little park and gazing across at the windows of No 1 for a glimpse of his first sweetheart, Fanny Balcombe. Perhaps, while watching a candle glow appear fitfully at one of the attic windows, the young Wilde pondered on the attic's contents — the bric-a-brac, the old, dusty, discarded paintings and portraits, changed and unchanging, old yet ageless. Was these the germ of an idea here — an idea that later flowered into the eerie novel *The Picture of Dorian Gray?* And what of the beautiful Fanny Balcombe?

'Then, turning to my love, I said,
The dead are dancing with the dead,
The dust is whirling with the dust.
But she — she heard the violin,
She left my side and entered in:
Love passed into the house of lust.'

Strange that Wilde should have lost the beautiful Miss Balcombe to another Dublin writer of the macabre, Bram Stoker. But then Stoker had the advantage of nearness. Fanny lived in No 1, he lived a few doors away at No 15. Wilde lived over the 'other side', in Merrion Square. Stoker was on the scene. Moreover, he possessed a more manly bearing and a far less complex character.

Whenever I pace through the Crescent on a dark night I imagine the young law clerk, Stoker, peering out from his drawing room window at the solitary figure of his unknown rival, the latter in a black cloak, his pale features luminous in the half light, his eyes dark and melancholy. While the future creator of Dorian Gray is gazing intently at the shadowy attics, might not the other watcher be peering down at an image in the swirling fog which may later become the black-cloaked Count Dracula?

A bell strikes midnight. The ghosts dissolve. The Crescent is now deserted. It is time for us to go....

Harmonstown/Raheny

'Raheny is a pleasant village of Dublin, surrounded by a beautiful tract of
pasture; its Church is on an eminence. All the roads from hence, through
the peninsula, are extremely sequestered and picturesque. Pop. 240.'
— Leigh's Road-Book of Ireland. 1832.

'Raheny is picturesquely situated amidst old trees on the brow of an
eminence crowned by a little church.'
— D'Alton's History of County Dublin. 1838.

When I travel out from the city by rail — especially nowadays on the
DART — I invariably take up a position on the left-hand side, facing the
driver's cabin, and, as we approach Raheny station, look out with a little
thrill of anticipation in the direction of St Joseph's Nursing Home, which,
since 1958, has been run by the excellent and kindly sisters of St Joseph of
Chambery. In my mind's eye I quickly eliminate the modern hospital
annexes and concentrate solely on the still discernible original building,
Edenmore House, formerly Violet Hall. And, with a kind of inward chuckle,
I allow myself to think: "Well now, Georgie Hoyte and Tommy Gresham,
what do you think of this for rail travel? Had you any idea?"

It is not too difficult for me to conjure up their ghosts standing on the
broad sweep of lawn before the house, frock-coated, and fob chains across
their silken waistcoats, balloon-shaped brandy glasses gently a-swish in their
pale unworkmanlike hands, cigar smoke wreathing their bare heads in the
waning sunlight of a May evening in 1844. Behind them the great windows
of Edenmore are ablaze with the warm glow from a score of chandeliers.
Through the open windows and the massive hall door the strains of a polka
— the latest craze! — pour out onto the crowded lawn. Dancing, swirling
couples can be glimpsed through the brilliant windows. On the expanse of
sunlit grass before the house there is a rustle of silk and velour as a bevy of
glossy-haired young ladies giggle with breathless excitement; they throng
about messers Hoyte and Gresham and the august figure of the Lord
Lieutenant. The latter, with fingers likewise caressing a brandy glass and a
good Havana, has his patrician head attentively inclined to one side as he
listens to Gresham and Hoyte, both of whom, with justifiable pride, are
boasting to the onlookers of their enterprise, explaining the mysteries of the
modern age of steam and rail travel, and confidently predicting a brave new
world of transport and communication. And why not? The brand new

Dublin to Drogheda Railway Company has just been inaugurated, the first sod having been cut just three years previously, right here in Raheny, almost directly below their vantage point on the lawn of Edenmore House. It is a proud moment for Hoyte and Gresham and the other promoters of the scheme, a cause for celebration and congratulations.

Earlier that day the inaugural train, on its return journey from Drogheda, had disgorged its fashionable passengers — the Viceroy and his entourage, the railway promoters, their families, their friends, their guests — at Raheny. There they had adjourned to Hoyte's former home, Edenmore, for a banquet and ball. They had dined well; the fulsome speeches and the liquid refreshment had been plentiful. Now, liveried servants are gliding amongst the guests on the lawn and the shadows are lengthening along the livid scar of earth that marks the railway escarpment just below. There is a chill in the air; it is time to go back in. The polka has given way to a Viennese waltz. On with the dance, let joy be unconfined!

Why not, indeed. The railway promoters were on to a good thing. Gresham, the Dublin hotelier who had already built extensively over in Kingstown, and who had foreseen the enormous benefits of easy access by rail to Dublin's surrounding beauty spots, was already anticipating an off-shoot of the Dublin-Drogheda line to carry passengers to Howth. George Hoyte, a wealthy 'drug-spice-and-colour' merchant with opulent premises in Sackville Street, and a recent Lord Mayor of Dublin to boot, had done very nicely by selling his Edenmore property to the railway company in which he held shares. All in all, it hadn't been a bad day's work.

And the unmitigated success of the venture did much to compensate Hoyte for his failed political campaign of mounting a last ditch stand against municipal reform. For more than 200 years the Corporation of Dublin had been a self-elective body, exclusively Protestant, and therefore effectively closed to Catholics and the 'lower orders'. But the Municipal Reform Bill of 1840 proposed to change all that by giving the franchise to citizens with a rateable valuation of £9 or over. Hoyte and his cronies were furious; he dashed off to London to present a petition at the bar of the House of Commons. He harangued the Tory leaders: 'The Municipal Corporations of Ireland are British in their origins and exclusively Protestant in their constitution ... the proposed Reform Bill ... destroys the exclusive Protestanism of the body. It substitutes a qualification by property for qualification by character — it lets in Popery and, therefore, it will ultimately swamp the Protestanism of the Corporation....'

But the Bill was passed. To add a tincture of salt to Hoyte's wounded bigotry in the next election he was displaced as Lord Mayor of Dublin by his arch-enemy Daniel O'Connell, the Catholic Liberator. Ah well, he at least had the consolation of concentrating more fully on his business affairs and of becoming more closely involved in the lucrative field of railroad speculation. What you lose on the roundabout of sectarian politics you pick up on the swings of commercial ventures!

An earlier Protestant owner of Edenmore House, Samuel Dick, who died in 1801, seems to have been a much more benign character. A wealthy Dublin merchant and a governor of the Bank of Ireland, in his will he left £30 yearly (payable from the rents of the eight charming cottages known as the Crescent, which he had earlier built to house servants and tenants of Edenmore) as an endowment for a school in Raheny 'for poor children of all religious persuasions'.

The Crescent cottages are still there — 200 years old, exquisitely pretty, with mullioned windows blinking southward at the sun, and only a few paces from the DART station. Right beside the Crescent stands the commodious Manhattan Bar; the first in a long line of hospitable inn-keepers was Felix McGowran, 'maker of jaunting cars, carts and agricultural implements', who built the tavern in 1844 in expectation of the railway custom, and who had his rent doubled as a result of defying the local Conservative caucus by urging his customers to vote for the Liberal candidate in the election of 1868.

Raheny is pre-eminently a village of churches. Directly opposite the Manhattan Bar, and lying in the centre of the village, is the 'church on an eminence' — or rather, the ruins of St Assam's church. The ruin also marks the site of the fort, or rath of Eanna, from which the locality takes its name. The church was built in 1712 on the site of an earlier church, each dedicated to the patron of Raheny, St Assam, a skilled metalworker said to be a disciple of St Patrick. A second St Assam's, built in the 1860s by one of the leading church architects of the day, Patrick Byrne, now serves as a community hall and stands at the opposite side of the Howth road to the present Roman Catholic Church of Our Lady, Mother of Divine Grace, an excellent example of modern Celtic architecture based on the Hiberno-Romanesque style.

Raheny's most interesting church is surely All Saints, the Church of Ireland parish church. An elaborate Victorian-gothic edifice of granite with limestone dressings, it has been likened to Salisbury Cathedral in miniature. Its arresting spire, octagonal in shape and with angle turrets, surmounts an imposing 3-stage tower and is a most impressively visible landmark for miles. Built in the 1880s, at a cost of £9,000, by Lord Ardilaun of the nearby St Anne's estate, his lordship also had a huge earthen bank raised along the roadside in a vain endeavour to deaden the noise emanating from Arthur McGowran's forge opposite the church. The blacksmith, suitably and financially compensated, was eventually induced to move his premises elsewhere. All Saints was designed by a prominent architect of the day, George Ashlin, and on its completion was praised for its 'perfectness of detail and general symmetry of its proportions, and in these particulars it is one of the most interesting churches in Ireland'.

But my favourite story relating to Raheny's churches concerns the earlier Protestant church and its graveyard. It was, in part, the setting for the macabre tale of a local man, John Lonergan, who, in 1781, as a consequence of being convicted of murdering his employer, was hanged and quartered on the Baggot Bridge gallows, was 'buried' in Raheny cemetery — and, within a month of his 'death', was sailing on the high seas to America. His trial was a *cause célèbre,* containing as it did all the lurid ingredients of a gothic melodrama — adultery, poison, a missing witness, protracted legal wranglings, the death sentence.

Lonergan has been educated at the Protestant school in Raheny and later at Trinity College. In 1777 he obtained the position of tutor at the home of Captain O'Flaherty, Castlefield, Co. Kilkenny. He also very quickly obtained the affections and favours of O'Flaherty's pretty young wife. There follows a brief, tempestuous love affair. Did the cuckolded captain suspect? What matter, within a few months he was dead of arsenic poisoning. And within days Lonergan was arrested and charged with murder. He vehemently protested his innocence — freely confessing the 'adulterous intrigue' with Mrs O'Flaherty, and, yes, freely admitting that he had once purchased arsenic at her behest, but swearing that she'd claimed it was intended for use on some verminous rats.

Very well then; fetch Mrs O'Flaherty, the examining magistrate snaps. But Mrs O'Flaherty cannot be found. She has vanished, gone overseas. Where? If Lonergan knows of her whereabouts he steadfastly refuses to reveal the facts. He must therefore face the consequences alone. He is charged with murder. There are various legal manoeuvres on both sides, delays, postponements; then the trial is switched from Kilkenny Assizes to Dublin. Why? For the titillation of a fashionable capital — or because Lonergan has dedicated friends there who are convinced of his innocence and are determined to assist him?

One such friend is his old mentor at Raheny, the Reverend Eugene McKenna. McKenna gives character testimony at the trial, but to no avail. He continues to visit Lonergan in jail right up to the very end. On the eve of execution he lingers till the very last moment in the condemned cell. There is much whispering, much low-voiced consultation as the clergyman advises his young friend on how to face the ordeal of the morrow, on how he should be prepared for ... for what?

Another such friend to the condemned man is Sergeant Porter of the Grenadier Company, a gallant body of men whom the sheriff has detailed to attend at the gallows on the following day. On leaving the prison McKenna hurries to Porter's house in Skinner's Row. The midnight candle gutters and dies over their whispered and urgent discussions. Are they planning something?

The fateful morning has arrived. Picture the scene: above the grey waters of the canal a stark gibbet stands on the stone bridge. There is a cart drawn up directly beneath the gallows. Lonergan, a hempen noose about his neck, stands on the cart, shivering in the sleety November wind. Porter's grenadiers form a tight square about the cart, holding back the huge throng of morbid onlookers. There is a deadly hush as the sheriff nods to the executioner. The cart is quickly pushed out from under Lonergan's feet. The awful silence is broken by a kind of savage yet mournful sigh. Here and there a head is bowed in prayer.

Some of the more experienced 'execution-goers' may perhaps have noticed that there was very little of the usual downward jerk-drop of the rope normally associated with such public hangings. In fact, the rope seems inordinately short for such a chore. Moreover, the condemned man almost immediately ceases to struggle and twitch in the air, and his life appears to be extinct in quicker time than is usual with such unfortunates. After about fifteen minutes — is this not a shorter duration than is customary? — someone calls for the 'poor craythur' to be cut down. Even as the sheriff accedes with a swift nod Porter has quickly drawn his sword and is barking an order for the cart to be brought once more under the swaying body. He jumps onto the cart, slashes upwards with his sword, severing the rope; and, with Reverend McKenna, quickly lowers the body onto the cart. At another signal from the sheriff the executioner steps forward with a sharp penknife and makes two small incisions in the shape of a cross on the nape of the dead man's neck — a mere formality this, a compliance with the legal requirement of 'quartering'.

McKenna and Porter place the body in a coffin and carry it to the clergyman's coach. The latter orders his coachman to make haste for Raheny churchyard. The crowd is dispersing. Once clear of the throng, the coachman applies the whip.

Dark curtains of icy rain shroud the little graveyard. There are not too many mourners about as the reverend gentleman conducts a brief service. The coffin is quickly lowered into what some eye-witnesses claim to be an exceptionally deep grave. To discourage body-snatchers, the Reverend McKenna explains. The same explanation is offered for his reason in mounting a guard over the freshly heaped clay of John Lonergan's burial place. Nobody is about to unearth this coffin and discover its secret.

Two days later Sergeant Porter is summoned to McKenna's home. He is lead upstairs and shown into a little-used attic. There, on a couch, is the man he so recently cut down from the gallow's rope — greatly shaken and debilitated, to be sure, but still very much alive. The 'miracle' of his survival is attributed to the unusually short rope, to the fact of his body having been swung sideways from the cart instead of receiving the usual short vertical drop, to having been cut free of the rope within a quarter of an hour, and — most of all — to the 'quartering' incisions, which had released blood from the neck. A series of fortunate coincidences — or an elaborately planned, if somewhat desperate, scheme to snatch their young friend from the jaws of death?

We shall never know for sure. What we do know is that a few nights later Lonergan was secretly removed to Porter's house where he hid for a week before being spirited aboard a ship bound for Bristol. From there, with a new identity as James Fennell, he sailed for America. There is another question that must forever remain unanswered: whatever became of the beautiful Mrs O'Flaherty who had 'vanished' abroad? Might not she have been waiting for her lover on the far side of the Atlantic?

Sutton

'We have now reached the district of Sutton, the threshold of Howth. Sutton Railway Station is situated at the narrowest point of the isthmus connecting Howth with the mainland, for it must be remembered that Howth is a land apart, at once a peninsula and a promontory. The development of Sutton, which comprises the isthmus and the western side of the Hill of Howth, has been quite phenomenal in the last twenty years. Nor can this be wondered at when we consider its great beauty and its mild climate. The latter is due to its sheltered position, the Hill acting as a barrier to the cold easterly breezes. This side of the Hill recalls the Mediterranean coast of Italy.'
  — North Dublin City and Environs. Dillon Cosgrave, 1909.

The coast of Italy? In places, perhaps.

Jonathan Swift would seem to have greatly appreciated the view on those summer mornings when he rode out along the seafront to visit his friends, Mrs Acheson at Grange House, or the Reverend Mr Webber, Vicar of Howth. The horseman's southward view, to his right, showed the splendid panorama of the bay and the Dublin mountains. To his left were the flat salt marshlands and the ruined church of Kilbarrack. The gravestones of the men 'who went down to the sea in ships' were dappled with sunlight, the ground carpeted with the softest grass and fern. Perhaps too there was a thin trickle of invisible water, a hidden rill finding its way out to the deep sigh of the sea. And behind the horseman lay the towers and chimneys and spires of the city.

Behind too lay tormented memories of Stella ... yes, and Vanessa ... the two women whom he loved, yet couldn't avoid wounding.

I never pass along the sea road at Sutton without seeing the ghost of the half-mad Dean cantering by, his eyes darting about, taking in his surroundings, noticing, not noticing, the head bowed one moment, then jerking up suddenly, the great mind constantly at work, pondering, balancing, sceptical, savagely indignant — a sad, tormented genius, the caverns of his tender and gloomy heart full of amorous perplexities.

There is no doubt that he loved both women in his own peculiar manner. Throughout his great London period (1708-13) he wrote almost daily to Stella, 'one of the most beautiful, graceful, and agreeable young women. Her hair was blacker than a raven, and every feature of her face in perfection', as he wrote, almost twenty years later, on the day of her death.

136

Thackeray tells us of that period that Swift "never sends away a letter to her but he begins a new one on the same day. He can't bear to let go her kind little hand, as it were. He knows that she is thinking of him, and longing for him far away in Dublin yonder. He takes her letters from under his pillow and talks to them, familiarly, paternally, with fond epithets and pretty caresses — as he would to the sweet and artless creature who loved him."

And yet some of those same letters wrung tears from Stella, for there was little attempt by Swift to keep all the happenings of his London sojourn from her. During his residence there he had made the acquaintance of a Mrs Vanhomrigh and her two daughters. With one of them, 'Vanessa', he once more had the opportunity and pleasure of tutoring a young woman of intellectual promise, as he had once tutored Stella. To Swift, liking to be admired and adored, this was a temptation he was apparently unable to resist. Both girls were much younger than the paternalistic dean, and fatherless. It had happened before, it was happening again. First there had been 'Varina' (Jane Waryng, the sister of a schoolmate when Swift was nineteen years old). Then 'Stella' (Esther Johnson) fifteen years when Swift was approaching thirty. And now 'Vanessa' (Hester Vanhomrigh) in her early twenties, when he was in his early forties. History does not record what became of 'Varina'. We know only too well the fate of 'Stella' and 'Vanessa'.

The latter, passionate and capricious, proved less amenable to Swift's platonic precepts than Stella had been. She fell in love with her mentor, happy to be thought his mistress while intending and planning to be his wife. It was all to end in bitter disappointment.

Swift was first to taste the bitterness. Hoping to be offered a bishopric by Queen Anne for his service to the Tory cause, he could do no more than extort from her ministers the deanery of St Patrick's, Dublin — an ecclesiastical dignity of no great value to him, requiring residence in a country he despised. He returned to Ireland, dispirited and angry. Vanessa's importunate letters pursued him. After a year she followed him to Ireland, insisting that they be married.

The whole business contained elements of scandal and comedy for the onlookers; for the participants — Swift and the two women who loved him — it was a tragedy. To the Dean the bitterest consequence was that he had brought such unhappiness to Stella. Thackeray says: "He had a sort of worship for her whilst he wounded her". To make amends he secretly married Stella. Unaware of this Vanessa continued to pursue him. In vain he protested, he vowed, he soothed, and he bullied. Sir Walter Scott tells us that 'her patience under this state of uncertainty for no less than eight years must have been partly owing to her awe for Swift, and partly, perhaps, to the weak state of her rival's health, which, from year to year, seemed to announce speedy dissolution.'

The patience finally snapped. Vanessa wrote to Stella, requesting to know the precise 'connection' with Dr Swift. And Stella, who likewise had remained outwardly calm and patient while inwardly experiencing hours of jealousy and quiet despair — Stella, who had been wounded to the very depths of her being! — was now ready to oblige her rival with the necessary information. She wrote, telling Vanessa of her secret marriage with the Dean. Vanessa was shattered.

Stella too was angry and full of resentment at Swift 'for having given another female such a right in him as Miss Vanhomrigh's inquiries implied'. She sent Vanessa's letter to Swift and, without waiting for a reply or being on hand to see him, retired to the house of a friend. Scott continues the tragic story:

'Swift, in one of those paroxysms of fury to which he was liable, both from temper and disease, rode instantly to Marley Abbey. As he entered the apartment, the sternness of his countenance, which was peculiarly formed to express the fiercer passions, struck the unfortunate Vanessa with such terror that she could scarce ask whether he would not sit down. He answered by flinging a letter on the table, and, instantly leaving the house, mounted his horse, and returned to Dublin. When Vanessa opened the packet she only found her own letter to Stella. It was her death-warrant. She sunk at once under the disappointment of the delayed yet cherished hopes which had so long sickened her heart, and beneath the unrestrained wrath of him for whom she had indulged them. How long she survived this last interview is uncertain, but the time does not seem to have exceeded a few weeks'.

A few weeks — hastened, it is rumoured, by heavy drinking. Poor Vanessa of the fevered, passionate, pursuing letters!

Before dying she cut Swift from her will and, as if still pursuing him vengefully, made arrangements for the publication of *Cadenus and Vanessa,* Swift's long poem celebrating their association and originally intended for Vanessa's eyes alone. Now all the world could read how he had wooed her.

Swift fled from Dublin at news of her death. And Stella, hearing that he had written beautifully of Vanessa, said with a smile: "That doesn't surprise me. For we all know the Dean could write beautifully about a broomstick."

Swift, meanwhile, busied himself with the *Drapier Letters* and the publication of *Gulliver's Travels.* And then — cruellest of blows! — Stella died in 1728. His world was left utterly and desolately empty. By this time also there were ominous signs that the curse of madness was about to afflict him — the terrible fits of dizziness and deafness which had assailed him from early manhood were about to destroy his mind. He had prophesied that he was to die first 'at top'. Three years before his death, in 1745, he was declared mentally incompetent and placed in charge of a keeper. And thirty years before that, when he was sent packing from London with his hopes dashed, he had complained that he was being sent to Ireland to die 'like a poisoned rat in his hole.'

But, as I said, whenever I travel along the sea road at Sutton I like to think of the Dean cantering along, enjoying the glories of a summer morning on his way to visit friends. For him these must have been rare moments of peace in his otherwise troubled and turbulent life. I like to think also of his wayward love for both Stella and Vanessa — yes, and even the forgotten Varina, and the half-remembered Lucy Gorges, Swift's 'blue-eyed nymph' who married the Lord of Howth in 1728. She once signed a letter to him — 'Your affectionate friend and sea-nymph. If I signed my name and the letter should be found, you and I might be suspected'.

The tangled romances and the copious letters brought out a side of the tortured Dean which should not be overlooked — a vein of tenderness and a capacity for eloquent affection at variance with most of his savage satires, a gentleness which is surprising and which is impossible to efface.

And there is a gentleness about Sutton in the evenings — especially those glorious Spring evenings such as we often get on this coast, when there is a suspicion of dew in the air which is yet not dampness, and a kind of warm glow foretelling of sunny days. Yes, this side of the Hill of Howth sometimes recalls the Mediterranean coast of Italy.

Around 3,500 B.C. Howth was an island and on its western shore — roughly where the boundary wall of Howth Demesne now touches modern Sutton — archaeologists have carried out extensive studies on an ancient midden, or pre-historic 'rubbish dump'. The studies reveal that the early Neolithic inhabitants were seashore dwellers, using crude stone implements of flint for their daily tasks. The midden contained shell, bone, charcoal and stone axeheads, evidence of the primitive hunting of wild boars, red deer, hares and of an equal reliance on fishing for sustenance.

There are only scant references to the locality prior to the 1800s, as its history is very closely intertwined with that of Howth in general. Ireland's earliest known census — that of Sir William Petty in 1659 — lists only 19 persons for Sutton, three 'English' and the remainder 'Irish'. The origins of the name are variously associated with John De Sutton (a 13th century kinsman of the Lords of Howth), with a corruption of the name 'south-town', or the Gaelic 'Suidhe Fhiontan', the Hill of Fintan, patron saint of the area. But as the Irish hagiologists list more than 25 saints of that name it is difficult to ascertain which Fintan is commemorated in the ruins of the 7th century church located in the old Sutton graveyard on the western base of Sheilmartin Hill. Nearby is the saint's holy well which is credited with curative powers.

In the 18th century Sutton was famous for its oyster beds. Together with Poolbeg, Clontarf and Malahide it provided an abundant supply of oysters to the capital. The beds were 'artificial', supplied with transplanted oysters from places as far apart as Portugal and France and with native oysters from Carlingford and Arklow. The development of Dublin port in the 19th century, and the resultant contamination from domestic sewage, sounded the death knell for the oyster beds about a hundred years ago.

Sutton quarries were also famous in the last century, providing everything from potters' clay, blue limestone, porphyry, manganese and 'marble as finely variegated as any in Egypt or Italy' to dolomite as a base material for such preparations as Epsom Salts and magnesiam limestone for 'bleaching salt of lime'. The once active quarries are long since gone, the land having been reclaimed for housing development which commenced in Sutton in the 1890s. The housing development — sporadic and gradual at first — gained impetus by the opening of a railway station at Sutton on the spur line connecting Howth with the main Dublin to Drogheda line. This spur, branching off at a quiet rural spot which became known as Howth Junction, was opened in 1847. It came about ten years too late — the hoped-for mail boat traffic had been diverted to Kingstown. In an effort to recoup some of the cost the directors offered bathing facilities and changing cubicles to holders of first class tickets and in general attempted to promote the area's scenic and maritime attractions as an inducement to day trippers.

Today's DART line, covering the same route, offers not only the same scenic and maritime attractions but a gateway to what Fr Dillon Cosgrave described as 'the most beautiful place near Dublin', an area rich in legend, lore and natural treasures. Just before my journey's end I can look out on Claremount's curve of golden sands and the waves breaking gently on the

Howth Village.

140

granite walls of Howth Harbour. Here, at the level crossing which is the entrance to the Howth Lodge Hotel I am reminded that the hotel is built on the site of the old 'Whiskey Forge', of which it was said that a Howthman, travelling homeward across the isthmus in the old days, never felt safe until he saw its welcoming lights.

Home ... safe ... welcoming lights ... whiskey ... the perfect end to my day of viewing from the DART.

And gently twirling a glass of translucent amber whiskey beside the fireside in any of Howth's excellent hostelries perhaps I will recall the words of another traveller of the old days, Daniel De Foe ... 'My journey cannot be barren of intelligence which way soever I turn; no, though I were to oblige myself to say nothing of anything that had been spoken of before'....

141

Bibliography

In addition to many old and not-so-old newspapers and magazines, local history pamphlets, CIE Public Affairs publications and journals of the Irish Railway Record Society the following books have been consulted and relied upon in the preparation of A view from the DART:

Leigh's Road-Book of Ireland. London. 1832.

The Four Georges and *The English Humorists.* William Makepeace Thackeray. London. Smith, Elder & Co. 1888.

The Book of Snobs. William Makepeace Thackeray. London & Glasgow. Collins' Clear-Type Press. 1910.

The Irish Sketch Book. William Makepeace Thackeray. London & Glasgow, Collins' Clear-Type Press. 1910.

North Dublin City and Environs. Dillon Cosgrave, O.Carm., B.A. Dublin. M. H. Gill and Son Ltd. 1909.

Life in Old Dublin. James Collins. (1913). Tower Books, Cork. (reprint) 1978.

After Thirty Years. Rt. Hon. The Viscount Gladstone. London. Macmillan and Co. 1928.

The Parish of Fairview. Rev. John Kingston, CC. Dundalk. Dundalgan Press (W. Tempest) Ltd. 1953.

The Phoenix Park Murders. Tom Corfe. London. Hodder & Stoughton. 1968.

Ireland Since the Famine. F. S. L. Lyons. London. Weidenfeld and Nicolson. 1971.

Faces of Old Leinster. Art O Broin and Sean McMahon. Belfast. Appletree Press. 1978.

The Heartland Heritage – North of the Liffey. Michael O Croinin. Dublin. Cll. Ray Fay, P.C., Publisher. 1978.

The Genius of Shaw. Michael Holroyd Ed. London. Hodder & Stoughton. 1979.

Where They Lived in Dublin. John Cowell. Dublin. O'Brien Press. 1980.

Ireland. Robert Kee. London. Weidenfeld and Nicolson. 1980.

Cahill's Dun Laoghaire Borough Guide and Directory (Centennial Year). Ed. Myles Tierney, M.P.R.I.I., M.C.C. FC Publications. Dublin. 1980.

Dun Laoghaire/Kingstown. Peter Pearson. Dublin. O'Brien Press. 1980.

Ireland's First Railway. K. A. Murray. Irish Railway Record Society. 1981.

The Howth Peninsula: Its History, Lore and Legend. Dublin. North Dublin Round Table. Ed. Vincent J. McBrierty. 1981.

The Villages of Dublin. Jimmy Wrenn. Dublin. Tomar Publishing Enterprises. 1982.

The Granite Hills. Published by Ballybrack ICA. Circa 1982.

Dublin. Benedict Kiely (Comp.). Oxford University Press. 1983.

Dubliners. James Joyce. Penguin Books. 1956.

Ulysses. James Joyce. Bodley Head. 1960.